CLEAN EATING

A 15-Day Meal Plan of Healthy Recipes for Weight Loss

Free Gift Included

As part of our commitment to making sure you live a healthy lifestyle, we have included a free e-book in the link below. This book informs of the food groups and food items that will enable you to lose weight quickly. I hope that you enjoy this e-book and the extra gift as well. The link to the gift is below:

http://36potentfoodstoloseweightandlivehealthy.gr8.com

Disclaimer

Copyright © 2016

All Rights Reserved.

No part of this eBook can be transmitted or reproduced in any form including print, electronic, photocopying, scanning, mechanical or recording without prior written permission from the author.

While the author has taken utmost efforts to ensure the accuracy of the written content, all readers are advised to follow information mentioned herein at their own risk. The author cannot be held responsible for any personal or commercial damage caused by information. All readers are encouraged to seek professional advice when needed.

About the Author

Sam Kuma is passionate about sharing his culinary experience with the world. His work involves the modernization of healthy diet plans. He has published many recipe books for vegan, ketogenic, paleo diets and dash food cooking, along with several cookbooks on ethnic cuisines. His main focus is to make healthy diets like vegan and ketogenic mainstream by sharing easy-to-create and appetizing recipes. In his first two books regarding vegan recipes, he has produced delicious vegan chocolates, desserts, ice creams, burgers, and sandwiches. Below is a link to his other Amazon products:

Sam Kuma Special

Book Description

The dieting trend that has recently taken the Internet by storm is the clean eating diet. However, unlike various other 'diet' trends, clean eating is much more than a fad diet. Clean eating is a healthy and refreshing lifestyle and not just another way of shedding those extra pounds. The best part about this diet is it can actually help you lose weight alongside reducing risks of various chronic diseases and disorders. It will also help you to regain your vigor and improve your overall health.

A lot of clean eating books exist in the market, so why this one? What makes it better compared to the others out there? Well, simply, this book is well researched; has well planned, tried and tested recipes and also includes a 15-day meal plan which will make it easier for you to follow through with your diet.

The objective of this book is to collect and present clean recipes to keep your taste buds happy and your tummy cheerful. I believe I was successful in this mission and can successfully welcome you to the world of clean eating. The meal plan consists of a new breakfast recipe, a fresh snack recipe and two additional meals that can help you lose weight.

The book is easy to refer to and features an in-depth index. The directions of the recipes are simple, clear and easy to follow so that even a beginner can cook them easily. I have tried to include recipes that can be made by almost everyone including college students, housewives, chefs, etc. The ingredients used are easily available and will not burn a hole in your pocket. You can also replace and exchange the ingredients - provided they are not processed. As mentioned earlier, clean eating is not a diet but a lifestyle; so this book is not a diet book. It is more of a recipe book that can help you achieve a healthy and fit body, all while eating your favorite foods.

Table of Contents

Free Gift Included 2

Disclaimer 3

About the Author 5

Book Description 6

Introduction 12

Chapter 1 – 15-Day Meal Plan 15

Chapter 2: Clean Eating Breakfast Recipes 22

    Marinara-Poached Eggs 22

    Cauliflower Pancakes 24

    Breakfast Smoothie Bowl 26

    Spinach Omelet Roll-Up 28

    Ricotta and Yogurt Parfait 30

    Breakfast Tacos 31

    Baked Denver Omelet 33

    Yellow Mellow 35

    Pizza Egg Muffins 36

Pumpkin-Papaya Acai Bowl 38

Banana Pancakes 40

Scrambled Tofu 42

Banana and Apple Bread 44

Super Foods Smoothie 47

Egg White and Avocado Bake 48

Chapter 3: Clean Eating Snack Recipes 49

Carrot with Avocado Dip 49

Strawberry Pops 50

Chili-Lime Spiced Pumpkin Seeds 52

Peanut Butter and Honey Oat Bars 54

Sweet Potato Fries 56

Southwestern Kale Chips 58

Spinach Rolls with Ricotta and Pistachios 60

Spicy Grilled Pineapple 62

Meatballs with Teriyaki Sauce 64

Mini Peanut Butter Sandwiches 66

Spiced Chickpea "Nuts" 67

Lettuce Wraps 69

Cucumber Boats 70

Crispy Edamame 71

Pita Pizza 72

Chapter 4: Clean Eating Lunch Recipes 75

Wild Salmon with Lentils and Arugula 75

Tofu Noodle Soup 77

Brown Rice Salad with Apples, Walnuts, and Cherries 81

One Pot Chicken and Broccoli Quinoa 83

Curried Shrimp 85

Quinoa Salad with Asparagus, Dates, and Orange 87

Mushroom Alfredo 89

Seafood Gazpacho 91

Chicken and Brown Rice Soup 93

Halibut Salad 95

Chicken with Brussels sprouts and Mustard Sauce 97

Chapter 5: Clean Eating Dinner Recipes 100

    Grilled Teriyaki Pork Lettuce Wraps........................ 100

    Sweet Potato Tofu Curry 102

    Creamy Risotto with Butternut Squash....................... 105

    Baked Chicken with Peppers and Mushrooms 108

    Thai Laksa Soup 110

    Roast Turkey Breast with Chipotle Chili Sauce 113

    Shepherd's Pie 115

    Grilled Pork Chops with Two-Melon Salsa................ 117

    Beef Stew.. 119

    Caribbean Chicken Salad.. 122

    Cruciferous Peanut Butter Rice 125

    Farmers Market Kale Tacos.. 128

Conclusion 130

Introduction

It is often said that you are what you eat and it is absolutely true: people who eat lots of fresh fruits and vegetables often appear vigorous and active. The above saying becomes even truer and more relevant in today's fast-food-obsessed world. So, unless you want to be greasy and overweight - stop eating fast food.

A person loses everything when they lose their health. It is our greatest asset as, without it; we cannot do anything. It is, therefore, essential to take care of your health. However, the amount of stress and pollution paired with our fast-paced life doesn't grant much time to look after ourselves. This often takes a toll on our health, and we end up sick. The best way to maintain our health is changing our lifestyle. One of the most basic changes is exchanging your fast food for clean food. But what is clean food?

Clean eating is a lifestyle change that is focused on food. We eat extreme amounts of junk food and processed food nowadays, thanks to our hectic schedules. Processed food includes any kind of food that has undergone some sort of 'process,' which increases the shelf life of the food. Oil, sugar, salts, and other processed chemicals fall under this category. Also, other foods like refined grains, which have been manufactured in a factory, can be called processed foods.

A clean eating plan is extremely healthy. It removes almost all processed items from your diet; making it one hundred percent natural. It can help you lose weight, enhance your skin tone, improve the quality of your hair, and make your bones strong and hard. It also improves digestion and your organ health such as your liver etc. It can also help to make your immune system strong and increase your immunity.

For those of you who have been eating processed foods, changing your lifestyle may seem like a herculean task; however, it is not impossible. Taking it slow can make the shift quite easy and pleasurable. To make the switch easier for you, I have collated a wide plethora of clean eating recipes that will sustain you for fifteen days.

The recipes are easy to cook and will help in your transitional phase and after.

The recipes are lip-smackingly delicious - all while healthy and nutrient-rich. The ingredients used are easy to find, cheap and unprocessed. These recipes will change the way you approach food and bring about a huge change in your health and fitness. So, what are we waiting for? Without further ado, let's get started.

Chapter 1 – 15-Day Meal Plan

Day 1

Breakfast - Marinara-Poached Eggs

Lunch - Wild Salmon with Lentils and Arugula

Snack - Carrot with Avocado Dip

Dinner - Grilled Teriyaki Pork Lettuce Wraps

Day 2

Breakfast - Cauliflower Pancakes

Lunch - Tofu Noodle Soup

Snack - Strawberry Pops

Dinner - Grilled Pork Chops with Two-Melon Salsa

Day 3

Breakfast - Breakfast Smoothie Bowl

Lunch - Brown Rice Salad with Apples, Walnuts, and Cherries

Snack - Spinach Rolls with Ricotta and Pistachios

Dinner - Roast Turkey Breast with Chipotle Chili Sauce

Day 4

Breakfast - Spinach Omelet Roll-Up

Lunch - Curried Shrimp

Snack - Crispy Edamame

Dinner - Caribbean Chicken Salad

Day 5

Breakfast - Ricotta and Yogurt Parfait

Lunch - Seafood Gazpacho

Snack - Peanut Butter and Honey Oat Bars

Dinner - Sweet Potato Tofu Curry

Day 6

Breakfast - Pumpkin-Papaya Acai Bowl

Lunch - Mushroom Alfredo

Snack - Meatballs with Teriyaki Sauce

Dinner - Farmers Market Kale Tacos

Day 7

Breakfast - Breakfast Tacos

Lunch - One Pot Chicken and Broccoli Quinoa

Snack - Spicy Grilled Pineapple

Dinner - Shepherd's Pie

Day 8

Breakfast - Baked Denver Omelet

Lunch - Chicken Taco Pizza

Snack - Chili-Lime Spiced Pumpkin Seeds

Dinner - Cruciferous Peanut Butter Rice

Day 9

Breakfast - Yellow Mellow

Lunch - Chicken and Brown Rice Soup

Snack - Spiced Chickpea "Nuts"

Dinner - Thai Laksa Soup

Day 10

Breakfast - Pizza Egg Muffins

Lunch - Quinoa Salad with Asparagus, Dates, and Orange

Snack - Sweet Potato Fries

Dinner - Baked Chicken with Peppers and Mushrooms

Day 11

Breakfast - Banana Pancakes

Lunch - Halibut Salad

Snack - Southwestern Kale Chips

Dinner - Creamy Risotto with Butternut Squash

Day 12

Breakfast - Banana and Apple Bread

Lunch - Chicken with Brussels Sprouts and Mustard Sauce

Snack - Mini Peanut Butter Sandwiches

Dinner - Beef Stew

Day 13

Breakfast - Scrambled Tofu

Lunch - Wild Salmon with Lentils and Arugula

Snack - Lettuce Wraps

Dinner - Grilled Pork Chops with Two-Melon Salsa

Day 14

Breakfast - Super Foods Smoothie

Lunch - One Pot Chicken and Broccoli Quinoa

Snack - Cucumber Boats

Dinner - Caribbean Chicken Salad

Day 15

Breakfast - Egg White and Avocado Bake

Lunch - Grilled Pork Chops with Two-Melon Salsa

Snack - Pita Pizza

Dinner - Farmers Market Kale Tacos

Chapter 2: Clean Eating Breakfast Recipes

Marinara-Poached Eggs

Prep: 5 min	Total: 15 min	Servings: 2

Ingredients:

- 2 eggs
- 4 teaspoons olive oil
- 1 small onion, thinly sliced
- ⅛ teaspoon red pepper flakes
- 2 small whole wheat pita pockets, toasted, chopped into wedges
- Salt to taste
- 1 cup marinara sauce

Instructions:

1. Place a skillet over medium heat. Add oil. When the oil is heated, add onions and sauté until light brown.

2. Add red pepper flakes, salt, and marinara sauce and heat thoroughly.
3. Crack the eggs into the skillet in 2 different places. Do not stir. Cover and cook until the eggs are cooked to the consistency you desire.
4. Serve with toasted whole-wheat pita wedges.

Cauliflower Pancakes

Prep: 10 min	Total: 30 min	Servings: 3

Ingredients:

- 1 large head cauliflower, broken into florets
- 3 tablespoons flat leaf parsley, chopped
- 3 eggs
- ¾ cup leeks, cleaned, chopped
- ¾ cup almond flour
- 2 cups smoked gouda cheese, shredded
- Salt to taste
- Pepper powder to taste
- 4-5 tablespoons coconut oil
- Eggs cooked sunny side up (for serving)

Instructions:

1. Place cauliflower florets in the food processor bowl and pulse until you get a coarse and rice-

like texture. Alternatively, you can grate it. Transfer into a bowl.
2. Place a skillet over medium heat. Add ½ tablespoon oil. When the oil is heated, add leeks and sauté until translucent.
3. Add garlic and sauté for a few seconds until fragrant. Remove from heat and transfer into the bowl of cauliflower.
4. Add parsley, salt, pepper, almond flour, eggs and Gouda cheese. Mix well.
5. Place a non-stick pan over medium heat. Add ½ teaspoon oil. When oil is heated, add about a spoonful of cauliflower mixture in the pan and spread a little using the back of a spoon.
6. Cook until the underside is golden brown. Flip sides and cook the other side too.
7. Remove onto a serving platter.
8. Repeat step 5 and 6 with the remaining batter.
9. Serve with eggs.

Breakfast Smoothie Bowl

Prep: 10 min	Total: 20 min	Servings: 2

Ingredients:

- 1 ½ cups nonfat plain Greek yogurt
- 2 cups frozen mango chunks
- ⅔ cup raspberries
- 1 ripe peach, pitted, sliced
- ½ cup low-fat milk
- 2 teaspoons chia seeds
- 2 tablespoons coconut flakes, toasted
- A handful of almonds, chopped, toasted
- 2 teaspoons vanilla extract

Instructions:

1. Add mango, yogurt, milk, and vanilla extract into a blender and blend until smooth.
2. Transfer into 2 serving bowls. Add chia seeds, raspberries and peach and stir. Chill if desired.

3. Sprinkle coconut flakes and almonds and serve.

Spinach Omelet Roll-Up

| Prep: 10 min | Total: 25 min | Servings: 2 |

Ingredients:

- 2 eggs, beaten
- 2 teaspoons olive oil or canola oil
- 2 teaspoons olive tapenade
- ⅛ teaspoon red pepper flakes
- 2 tablespoons goat's cheese, crumbled
- Salt to taste
- 2 cups baby spinach, torn

Instructions:

1. Place a skillet over medium heat. Add 1 teaspoon of oil. When the oil is heated, add half the beaten egg and swirl the skillet. Cook until the underside is done. Flip sides and cook for a minute. Transfer onto a plate.
2. Repeat the above step with the remaining egg.

3. Place the skillet back on heat and add spinach. Cook until the spinach wilts. Remove from heat.
4. Spread 1 teaspoon of tapenade onto each of the cooked eggs.
5. Sprinkle half the goat's cheese and half the spinach onto each. Sprinkle chili flakes and salt.
6. Roll up and serve with a dip of your choice.

Ricotta and Yogurt Parfait

Prep: 10 min	Total: 15 min	Servings: 2

Ingredients:

- ½ cup part semi-skimmed, ricotta cheese
- 1 ½ cups non-fat vanilla Greek yogurt
- ½ cup raspberries of any other berries of your choice
- 1 teaspoon lemon zest, grated
- 2 teaspoons chia seeds
- 2 tablespoons almonds, slivered

Instructions:

1. Add yogurt, ricotta cheese and lemon zest into a bowl and stir.
2. Divide and pour into 2 parfait glasses. Chill if desired
3. Sprinkle chia seeds, raspberries, and almonds on top and serve.

Breakfast Tacos

Prep: 10 min	Total: 20 min	Servings: 4

Ingredients:

- 8 large eggs, lightly beaten
- 1 large onion, chopped
- 2 tablespoons extra virgin olive oil
- 4 cloves garlic, minced
- 12 medium tomatillos, husked, rinsed, coarsely chopped
- Salt to taste
- Pepper powder to taste
- ½ cup feta cheese, crumbled
- 8 small corn or whole wheat tortillas or taco shells

Instructions:

1. Place a skillet over medium heat. Add oil. When the oil is heated, add tomatillos, onion, and garlic and cook until almost dry.
2. Add eggs, salt and pepper. Stir and cook until the eggs are set.
3. Warm the tortillas, if desired, according to the instructions on the package.
4. Divide the mixture into the tortillas or taco shells. Garnish with cheese and serve.

Baked Denver Omelet

Prep: 15 min	Total: 45 min	Servings: 3

Ingredients:

- 4 large eggs
- 1 small onion, finely chopped
- ¼ cup green bell pepper, finely chopped
- ¼ cup red bell pepper, finely chopped
- 2 teaspoons olive oil
- ½ cup cooked ham, chopped
- 3 tablespoons milk
- ¼ cup low-fat cheddar cheese, shredded
- A dash of hot sauce to serve
- Chopped chives to serve
- Avocado slices to serve (optional)
- Salt to taste
- Pepper powder to taste

Instructions:

1. Place a skillet over medium-high heat. Add oil. When the oil is heated, add onion, and bell peppers and sauté until the vegetables are soft. Remove from heat.
2. Place the ham pieces in a small, greased baking dish (6X6 inches). Place the cooked vegetables on top of it.
3. Sprinkle cheese over it.
4. Whisk together eggs, salt, pepper, and milk in a bowl and pour over the cheese in the baking dish.
5. Bake in a preheated oven at 400° F until set. Slice into wedges.
6. Sprinkle chives, dot with hot sauce and serve with an avocado slice if desired.

Yellow Mellow

Prep: 10 min	Total: 12 min	Servings: 4

Ingredients:

- 1 ½ cups fresh, ripe mango, pitted, peeled, chopped into chunks
- 3 medium bananas, peeled, sliced, frozen
- 2 ½ cups water
- 3 tablespoons raw almond butter
- 1/3 cup raw hemp seeds, hulled
- 1 ½ teaspoons vanilla extract
- 1 ½ tablespoons honey
- A pinch of salt

Instructions:

1. Add all the ingredients into a blender and blend until smooth.
2. Serve in tall glasses with crushed ice.

Pizza Egg Muffins

| Prep: 10 min | Total: 45 min | Servings: 6 |

Ingredients:

- ½ cup broccoli, chopped, cooked
- 4 large eggs
- 4 ounces sliced mushrooms
- 1 tablespoon coconut milk or skim milk
- 2 tablespoons black olives, sliced
- 1 teaspoon canola oil
- ½ tablespoon pizza seasoning
- ¼ teaspoon salt or to taste
- ¼ teaspoon pepper powder or to taste

Instructions:

1. Place a skillet over medium-high heat. Add oil. When the oil is heated, add mushrooms and sauté until light brown. Remove from heat; add broccoli and olives and stir.

2. Place a little of this mixture into a lined and greased muffin tray to fill about ¼ each.
3. Whisk together eggs, milk, pizza seasoning, salt, and pepper in a bowl. Pour this mixture into the muffin tray over the vegetables so as to fill up to ⅔ each.
4. Place the muffin tray in a preheated oven and bake at 350° F for 20-25 minutes or until a toothpick, when inserted in the center of the muffin, comes out clean.

Pumpkin-Papaya Acai Bowl

Prep: 10 min	Total: 15 min	Servings: 6

Ingredients:

For the acai bowl:
- 1 cup papaya
- 1 cup canned pumpkin
- 2 medium bananas, sliced
- 2 frozen acai smoothie pack, unsweetened
- 1 tablespoon ground cinnamon
- 1 tablespoon pumpkin pie spice
- 2 tablespoons maca powder
- 2 cups almond milk

To serve:
- 1 cup goji berries
- ½ cup cashews, chopped, toasted
- A few slices of papaya
- A few slices of banana

- ½ cup pomegranate seeds
- ½ cup granola

Instructions:

1. Add all the ingredients of the acai bowl into the blender and blend until smooth. Pour into 6 serving bowls. Chill if desired.
2. Add papaya, banana, and pomegranate seeds and stir.
3. Sprinkle goji berries, cashews, and granola on top and serve.

Banana Pancakes

Prep: 10 min	Total: 25 min	Servings: 2-3

Ingredients:

- ¾ cup quick cooking oats
- 2 tablespoons 1% cottage cheese, unsalted
- 6 egg whites
- 1 small banana, peeled, chopped
- 1 teaspoon vanilla extract
- 2 tablespoons walnuts, chopped
- ½ teaspoon ground cinnamon
- 2 tablespoons coconut oil or more if required

Instructions:

1. Add all the ingredients, except coconut oil, into a blender and blend until smooth. Transfer into a bowl. If you find the batter too watery, then add a little oat flour and stir.

2. Place a nonstick pan over medium heat. Add about a teaspoon of coconut oil. When the oil melts, add about ¼ cup of the batter. Swirl the pan slightly so that the batter spreads.
3. Cook until the underside is golden brown. Flip sides and cook the other side too. Remove from the pan and keep warm.
4. Repeat the above 2 steps with the remaining batter.
5. Serve warm with a drizzle of honey or agave nectar.

Scrambled Tofu

| Prep: 10 min | Total: 25 min | Servings: 4 |

Ingredients:

- 2 tablespoons olive oil
- 2 bunches green onions, chopped, place the white parts and green parts separately
- 2 large tomatoes, chopped
- 2 packages (12 ounces each) firm silken tofu, drained, crumbled
- ½ teaspoon ground turmeric
- Salt to taste
- Pepper powder to taste
- ½ teaspoon red chili flakes
- 1 cup cheddar cheese, shredded (optional)
- Any other seasoning of your choice (optional)

Instructions:

1. Place a skillet over medium heat. Add oil. When the oil is heated, add whites of the onions. Sauté until translucent.
2. Add turmeric, salt, red chili flakes, pepper and any seasonings of your choice, if using. Sauté for a few seconds until fragrant.
3. Add tomatoes and cook for 4-5 minutes
4. Add tofu and onion greens and stir.
5. Lower heat and let it heat thoroughly. Sprinkle cheddar cheese, if using, and serve.

Banana and Apple Bread

Prep: 15 min	Total: 1 hr. 15 min	Servings: 6-8

Ingredients:

For the banana bread:
- 2 cups oat bran
- 2 cups almond meal
- 1 cup extra light olive oil
- ½ teaspoon ground nutmeg
- 2 teaspoons baking powder
- 4 tablespoons stevia powder
- 1 teaspoon ground cinnamon
- 6 over-ripe bananas, mashed
- ½ cup almond milk
- 1 teaspoon vanilla extract
- 4 eggs

For the apples:

- 4 Granny Smith apples, peeled, cored, chopped
- 1 teaspoon ground cinnamon
- 2 tablespoons stevia
- 1 teaspoon vanilla extract

Instructions:

1. To cook the apples: Add apples, vanilla extract, stevia, and cinnamon to a pan and place over medium heat. Cook until golden brown. Remove from heat and set aside.
2. To make the banana bread: Add all the dry ingredients into a large bowl and stir.
3. Add oil, eggs, almond milk and vanilla to a bowl and whisk well.
4. Pour into the dry ingredients mixture a little at a time. Stir until well-combined each time.
5. Add bananas and stir.
6. Add apple mixture and fold gently.
7. Pour the batter into a greased loaf pan.

8. Bake in a preheated oven at 350° F for about 50 minutes or until a toothpick, when inserted in the center, comes out clean.
9. Cool completely.
10. Slice and serve.

Super Foods Smoothie

Prep: 10 min	Total: 12 min	Servings: 4

Ingredients:

- 2 small bananas, peeled, sliced, frozen
- 2 cups baby spinach
- 2 cups frozen berries of your choice
- 1 inch fresh ginger, peeled, sliced
- 2 cups chilled green tea
- 1 cup kefir or low-fat plain Greek yogurt
- 1 cup pomegranate juice

Instructions:

1. Add all the ingredients into a blender and blend until smooth.
2. Serve in tall glasses with crushed ice.

Egg White and Avocado Bake

Prep: 5 min	Total: 20 min	Servings: 4

Ingredients:

- 10 egg whites
- 1 tablespoon butter, unsalted
- 2 ripe Hass avocados, peeled, pitted, sliced
- Salt to taste
- Pepper powder to taste

Instructions:

1. Whisk egg whites with salt and pepper. Add half the avocado slices.
2. Grease a baking dish with butter. Pour the egg white mixture into it.
3. Bake in a preheated oven at 375° F for about 15 minutes or until set.
4. Chop into wedges and serve with the remaining avocado slices.

Chapter 3: Clean Eating Snack Recipes

Carrot with Avocado Dip

Prep: 10 min	Total: 12 min	Servings: 6-8

Ingredients:

- 2 ripe avocados, peeled, pitted, chopped
- 3 cups snow peas, shelled, steamed, cooled
- 2-3 tablespoons lime juice
- 2 cloves garlic, halved
- Salt to taste
- ½ teaspoon cayenne pepper
- Carrots peeled, chopped into finger like sticks

Instructions:

1. Add all the ingredients, except carrots, into the blender and blend until smooth.
2. Transfer into individual serving bowls.
3. Serve with carrot sticks.

Strawberry Pops

Prep: 10 min	Total: 20 min + freezing time	Servings: 12

Ingredients:

- 1 ½ cups pineapple juice
- 6 cups strawberries, hulled, halved
- 2 ripe bananas, peeled, chopped
- 6 tablespoons honey.

Instructions:

1. Place a saucepan over medium heat. Add strawberries and pineapple juice and simmer for 5-6 minutes.
2. Remove from heat and cool completely.
3. Transfer into a blender along with the bananas and blend until smooth.
4. Fill into Popsicle molds. Place sticks in each mold and freeze.

5. Remove from the molds and serve.

Chili-Lime Spiced Pumpkin Seeds

Prep: 5 min	Total: 20 min	Servings: 12

Ingredients:

- 6 cups raw pumpkin seeds (pepitas)
- 2 tablespoons butter or ghee, melted (optional)
- 2 teaspoons cayenne pepper
- 2 teaspoons chili powder or to taste
- 1 ½ teaspoons sea salt
- ⅓ cup fresh lemon juice

Instructions:

1. Place the pepitas in a baking dish. Add ghee, lemon juice, cayenne pepper, chili powder, sea salt and cayenne pepper and toss well.
2. Bake in a preheated oven at 275° F for about 10-15 minutes or until done. Cool and store in an airtight container in the refrigerator.

Note: You can also make spicy nuts using the same ingredients replacing pumpkin seeds with nuts of your choice.

Peanut Butter and Honey Oat Bars

Prep: 5 min	Total: 10 min	Servings: 8

Ingredients:

- ¼ cup honey-roasted peanuts, chopped
- ¼ cup honey
- 3 tablespoons peanut butter
- 2 teaspoons coconut oil
- ¼ teaspoon ground cinnamon
- ¼ teaspoon vanilla extract
- 1 cup oats

Instructions:

1. Line a small baking pan with parchment paper so that the paper is hanging over the sides.
2. Add honey, oil, and peanut butter into a microwave-safe bowl. Microwave for 20 -30 seconds or until the peanut butter melts completely.

3. Remove from the microwave and add rest of the ingredients. Mix well and pour into the baking pan. Spread the mixture and press with the back of a spoon.
4. Bake in a preheated oven 300° F for about 20 minutes or until the top is light brown in color.
5. Remove from the oven and press once again.
6. Cool for a while and slice.
7. Cool completely and serve.

Sweet Potato Fries

Prep: 10 min	Total: 40 min	Servings: 4

Ingredients:

- 4 medium sweet potatoes, peeled, sliced into julienne strips
- 1 teaspoon chili powder
- 1 teaspoon pepper powder
- 1 teaspoon cumin powder
- ½ teaspoon cayenne pepper
- Sea salt to taste
- 2 tablespoons extra virgin olive oil

Instructions:

1. Add all the ingredients into a bowl and toss well.
2. Transfer onto a greased baking sheet, making a single layer.
3. Bake in a preheated oven 425° F for about 30 minutes or until the top is light brown in color. It

should be tender inside and crisp outside. Turn the sweet potatoes half-way through baking.

Southwestern Kale Chips

Prep: 15min	Total: 45 min	Servings: 3-4

Ingredients:

- 2 bunches kale leaves, discard hard stems and ribs, rinsed, drained, pat dried, torn
- Cooking spray
- Salt to taste
- ½ teaspoon pepper powder
- 1 teaspoon cayenne pepper
- 1 teaspoon chili powder
- ¼ teaspoon garlic powder
- 1 teaspoon cumin powder
- 4 teaspoons apple cider vinegar
- Cooking spray

Instructions:

1. Add all the ingredients, except kale, to a bowl and sprinkle it over the kale. Spray with cooking spray. Keep aside for a while.
2. Spread the leaves on a greased baking sheet.
3. Bake in a preheated oven at 250° F for about 20 minutes or until crisp.
4. Remove from the oven and transfer to a plate lined with paper towels.
5. Cool completely and store in an airtight container.

Note: You can replace kale with the leaves of Brussels sprouts or zucchini slices.

Spinach Rolls with Ricotta and Pistachios

Prep: 10 min	Total: 25 min	Servings: 8

Ingredients:

- 4 tablespoons extra-virgin olive oil, divided
- 18 ounces fresh spinach, rinsed, discard tough stems, finely chopped
- 14 ounces part skim ricotta
- ½ cup low fat parmesan cheese, grated, divided
- 1 teaspoon ground nutmeg
- 8 whole wheat lasagna sheets, cook according to the instructions on the package
- 2 cups pistachio nuts, finely chopped
- Salt to taste

Instructions:

1. Place a skillet over medium heat. Add half the oil. When the oil is heated, add spinach and salt

and sauté until the spinach wilts. Remove from heat and cool completely. Transfer into a bowl.
2. Add ricotta, half the Parmesan, nutmeg, pistachio nuts, and salt and set aside.
3. Pat dry the cooked lasagna sheets. Place a lasagna sheet on your work area.
4. Spread the cheese mixture over it. Roll and set aside.
5. Repeat with the remaining mixture and lasagna sheets.
6. Cut into 1-2 inch slices.
7. Drizzle the remaining oil over it and sprinkle the remaining cheese on top and serve as it is or microwave for a few seconds until the cheese melts and then serve.

Spicy Grilled Pineapple

| Prep: 10 min | Total: 15 min + chilling time | Servings: 6-8 |

Ingredients:

- 2 cans (8 ounces each) unsweetened pineapple slices (you can use fresh pineapple slices too)
- 2 large jalapenos, deseeded, minced
- Juice of 2 limes
- ¼ teaspoon cayenne pepper
- ½ teaspoon chili powder
- Salt to taste

Instructions:

1. Preheat a grill and grill the pineapple pieces on both sides until brown.
2. Once cool enough to handle, chop the pineapple slices into bite-sized pieces. Transfer into a bowl.

3. Add rest of the ingredients. Mix well. Cover and refrigerate for about an hour before serving. Stir in a couple of times while it is chilling.

Meatballs with Teriyaki Sauce

Prep: 20 min	Total: 45 min	Servings: 8

Ingredients:

- 2 pounds lean ground beef or turkey
- 4 tablespoons honey
- 5 tablespoons light soy sauce
- 4 tablespoons rice wine vinegar
- 4 slices whole wheat bread, discard the crusts
- 1 onion, minced
- 2 green onions, chopped for garnishing
- ½ cup milk
- 2 tablespoons sesame seeds, toasted plus extra for garnishing
- Salt to taste
- Pepper powder to taste
- 2 tablespoons sesame oil
- ¼ cup olive oil
- 2 eggs

Instructions:

1. To make teriyaki sauce: Mix together soy sauce, honey and rice wine vinegar in a bowl and set aside.
2. Place bread slices in a bowl. Pour milk over it. Set aside for a few minutes and then squeeze the bread so that the excess milk drains off.
3. Mix together in a large bowl the rest of the ingredients except olive oil. Add bread and mix well using your hands.
4. Make small balls of the mixture and set aside.
5. Place a nonstick skillet over medium heat. Add 3 tablespoons of olive oil. When the oil is heated, add the meatballs and cook until brown on all the sides. If the pan gets too crowded, then cook the meatballs in batches.
6. Add teriyaki sauce and mix well. Heat thoroughly.
7. Garnish with green onions and sesame seeds. Fix toothpicks in the balls and serve immediately.

Mini Peanut Butter Sandwiches

| Prep: 10 min | Total: 15 min | Servings: 6 |

Ingredients:

- 2 large banana, sliced evenly (about 30 slices)
- 6 medium strawberries, sliced evenly (about 15 slices)
- 3 tablespoons peanut butter

Instructions:

1. Spread 15 banana slices over a plate and spread the peanut butter over each of them.
2. Lay a slice of strawberry on each of the 15 buttered bananas.
3. Cover each with the remaining 15 slices of banana.
4. Mini peanut butter sandwiches are ready to serve.

Spiced Chickpea "Nuts"

| Prep: 5 min | Total: 50 min | Servings: 6-8 |

Ingredients:

- 2 cans (15 ounces each) chickpeas, rinsed or use equivalent amount of cooked chickpeas, pat dried
- 4 teaspoons ground cumin
- ½ teaspoon ground allspice
- 2 teaspoons dried marjoram
- 2 tablespoons olive oil
- ½ teaspoon salt or to taste

Instructions:

1. Add all the ingredients to a bowl and toss until the chickpeas are well coated.
2. Transfer onto a rimmed baking sheet.
3. Bake in a preheated oven at 250° F for about 25-30 minutes or until crisp.

4. Remove from the oven and transfer to a plate lined with paper towels.
5. Cool completely and store in an airtight container.

Lettuce Wraps

Prep: 5 min	Total: 15 min	Servings: 4

Ingredients:

- 8 leaves iceberg lettuce
- 4 slices roast turkey
- ½ cucumber, sliced
- 1 tomato, sliced
- Hummus as required
- ¼ teaspoon paprika
- Salt to taste

Instructions:

1. Spread 4 lettuce leaves on your working area.
2. Place a slice of turkey on 4 of the leaves.
3. Lay a few slices of cucumber and tomatoes. Add a dollop of hummus. Sprinkle paprika and salt.
4. Fold over and wrap another lettuce leaf all over it.

Cucumber Boats

Prep: 10 min	Total: 12 min	Servings: 4

Ingredients:

- 2 cucumbers, peeled, cut into 2 (lengthwise), deseeded
- 5-6 tablespoons hummus or as required
- 8 baby tomatoes, sliced
- A handful of arugula
- 1 carrot, shredded
- Pepper powder to taste
- Salt to taste

Instructions:

1. Spread hummus on the inside of the cucumber boats. Spread arugula, carrots, and tomatoes over it.
2. Season with salt and pepper and serve.

Crispy Edamame

| Prep: 5 min | Total: 50 min | Servings: 2 |

Ingredients:

- 8 ounces frozen edamame, shelled, thawed
- 2 teaspoons lemon juice
- 2 teaspoons olive oil
- Salt to taste
- Pepper to taste

Instructions:

1. Place edamame in a bowl. Add oil and lemon juice.
2. Place on a foil-lined baking sheet and bake in a preheated oven at 375° F for about 45 minutes or until light brown and crisp.
3. Remove from oven and sprinkle salt and pepper immediately. Cool completely and store in an airtight container.

Pita Pizza

Prep: min	Total: min	Servings: 4-6

Ingredients:

For Pizza:
- 2 whole wheat pita breads
- 1 ½ ounces mozzarella cheese, grated
- ½ a yellow bell pepper, deseeded, chopped into thin strips

For the tomato sauce:
- 1 small yellow onion, peeled, chopped into 1cm pieces
- 1 small bay leaf
- 7 ounces canned whole tomatoes, peeled, chopped
- ½ teaspoon olive oil

- 1 clove garlic, peeled, minced
- ¼ teaspoon dried basil
- ¼ teaspoon dried oregano
- ¼ teaspoon crushed red pepper flakes
- 2 tablespoons tomato paste

Instructions:

1. To make the tomato sauce: Place a pan over medium heat. Add oil. When the oil is heated, add onion and garlic and sauté until brown.
2. Add oregano, basil, bay leaf, red pepper flakes, tomatoes, and tomato paste.
3. Mix well and bring to a boil.
4. Lower heat to medium-low and let it simmer for a while until the liquid is dried up. Discard the bay leaf
5. Place pita bread on a baking sheet. Divide and spread tomato sauce over it. Sprinkle bell pepper strips followed by mozzarella cheese.
6. Bake in a preheated oven at 350° F for about 20 minutes or until the cheese melts.

7. Remove the pizzas from the oven and transfer onto your work area. Garnish with basil, cut each pizza into 12 slices and serve.

Chapter 4: Clean Eating Lunch Recipes

Wild Salmon with Lentils and Arugula

Prep: 10 min	Total: 1 hr. 20 min	Servings: 6

Ingredients:

- 1 ½ cups green lentils, rinsed, soaked in water for 5-6 hours
- 6 fillets (6 ounces each) wild salmon, skinless
- 5 cups baby arugula
- 2 stalks celery, chopped
- 2 carrots, peeled, diced
- 1 large onion, chopped
- 2 bay leaves
- 3 tablespoons extra virgin olive oil plus extra for drizzling
- 2 tablespoons lemon juice
- Sea salt to taste
- Pepper powder to taste

Instructions:

1. Add onions, carrots, celery, bay leaf and lentils to a large pot and place it over medium heat. Bring to the boil.
2. Lower heat, cover and cook until tender. Drain and set aside. Add salt, pepper, oil and lemon juice, and arugula, mix well, cover and set aside.
3. Place the fillets in a baking dish. Drizzle olive oil and sprinkle salt and pepper. Cover with aluminum foil.
4. Bake in a preheated oven at 375° F until done. Unwrap.

Tofu Noodle Soup

Prep: min	Total: min	Servings: 8

Ingredients:

- 9 cups water
- 3 cups tofu, chopped
- 3 carrots, peeled, chopped
- 10 green beans, chopped into ½ cm pieces
- 1 green bell pepper, chopped
- 1 red bell pepper, chopped
- 2 cups cabbage, chopped
- 1 ½ cups fresh or frozen corn
- ½ cup parsley, chopped
- 5 stalks celery, chopped
- 10 tablespoons vegetarian broth powder
- 1 ½ teaspoons sea salt or Himalayan salt
- 1 teaspoon pepper powder
- A dash of hot sauce to serve

- ¾ box quinoa spaghetti noodles, broken into 2-inch pieces

Instructions:

1. Add all the ingredients, except noodles, to a soup pot or large saucepan. Place the saucepan over medium heat. Bring to the boil.
2. Lower heat, cover and simmer until the vegetables are tender.
3. Add noodles and cook until the noodles are al dente.
4. Ladle into individual soup bowls. Add a dash of hot sauce and serve immediately.

Chicken Taco Pizza

| Prep: 15 min | Total: 45 min | Servings: 8 |

Ingredients:

- 2 whole wheat pizza crusts, freshly made or frozen
- 2 frozen chicken breasts, skinless, boneless, thawed, chopped into bite-sized pieces
- 2 cups frozen corn, thawed
- 2 cups cooked black beans, rinsed, drained
- 1 cup salsa plus extra to serve
- 2 cups semi-skimmed mozzarella cheese, grated, divided
- ½ cup fresh cilantro, chopped

Instructions:

1. Lay the pizza crusts on a large baking sheet. Divide salsa and spread over both the crusts. Sprinkle half the cheese over the salsa.

2. Sprinkle beans, corn, and chicken over the cheese. Finally, top with the remaining half cheese.
3. Bake in a preheated oven 425° F until the cheese is melted and slightly brown.
4. Remove from the oven and sprinkle cilantro on it. Cut into wedges and serve with some more salsa.

Brown Rice Salad with Apples, Walnuts, and Cherries

Prep: 15 min	Total: 45 min	Servings: 4-5

Ingredients:

- 2 cups brown rice, rinsed, cooked according to the instructions on the package
- 2 apples, diced into ½ inch pieces
- 1 ½ cups frozen peas, thawed
- ⅔ cup walnuts, chopped
- ½ cup dried cherries, roughly chopped
- 2 bunch chives, finely chopped

For dressing:
- 4 cloves garlic, minced
- 2 tablespoons agave syrup
- 4 tablespoons canola oil
- ½ cup sesame seeds, toasted
- 2 teaspoons yellow miso paste

- 4 tablespoons balsamic vinegar

Instructions:

1. Fluff the cooked rice and cool completely.
2. Mix together all the ingredients for the salad in a large bowl. Add rice and toss well.
3. To make the dressing: Mix together all the ingredients for the dressing. Whisk well.
4. Pour over the salad. Toss well and serve.

One Pot Chicken and Broccoli Quinoa

Prep: 15 min	Total: 40 min	Servings: 3

Ingredients:

For the chicken:
- 1 pound chicken breasts, skinless, boneless, chopped into 1-inch pieces
- ½ teaspoon ground allspice
- ½ teaspoon Himalayan pink salt
- ¼ teaspoon ground cumin
- ½ tablespoon olive oil
- Black pepper powder to taste
- Salt to taste

For quinoa:
- ¾ cup quinoa, rinsed
- ½ cups hot water
- 1 medium onion, chopped
- 1 medium carrot, peeled, shredded

- 2 cloves garlic, minced
- ½ teaspoon extra virgin olive oil
- ½ pound broccoli, chopped into florets
- 1 bay leaf

Instructions:

1. Place a deep skillet over medium-high heat. Add all the ingredients of the chicken and cook until golden brown. Transfer into a bowl.
2. Place the skillet back on the heat. Add oil, onions, garlic and carrots and sauté for around 5 minutes.
3. Add chicken and all the ingredients of the quinoa except broccoli and cook until the water is almost dried up.
4. Add broccoli and stir.
5. Lower heat, cover and cook for 4-5 minutes.
6. Serve hot. Leftovers can be refrigerated in an airtight container for a couple of days.

Curried Shrimp

Prep: 15 min	Total: 30 min	Servings: 6

Ingredients:

- 2 pounds large shrimp, peeled
- 2 medium onions, chopped
- 1 cup tomatoes, pureed
- 8 cloves garlic, minced
- 4 teaspoons ginger, minced
- 1 teaspoon ground turmeric
- 1 teaspoon ground cumin
- 1 teaspoon ground coriander
- 2 bunches fresh cilantro, minced
- ⅓ cup lime juice
- 4 tablespoons olive oil

Instructions:

1. Place a large saucepan over medium heat. Add oil. When oil is heated, add onions and garlic and sauté until onions are translucent.
2. Add tomatoes, ginger, cumin, coriander, and turmeric and mix well.
3. Lower heat and simmer for 5-6 minutes. Add shrimp and cook until done. Add cilantro and stir.
4. Remove from heat. Stir in lime juice and serve over cooked brown rice.

Quinoa Salad with Asparagus, Dates, and Orange

Prep: 15 min	Total: 45 min	Servings: 2-3

Ingredients:

- ½ cup quinoa, uncooked
- ¼ cup white onion, finely chopped
- ½ cup orange segments, deseeded, chopped
- ¼ pound asparagus, sliced, steamed, cooled
- 1 cup water
- 2 tablespoons pecans, toasted
- 1 tablespoon red onion, minced
- 3 dates, pitted, chopped
- ¼ teaspoon kosher salt or to taste
- ½ jalapeño pepper, sliced
- ½ teaspoon olive oil

For dressing:
- 1 tablespoon fresh lemon juice
- 1/2 tablespoon extra virgin olive oil

- 1 clove garlic, minced
- ⅛ teaspoon kosher salt or to taste
- ⅛ teaspoon black pepper
- A handful of mint leaves, chopped and a few sprigs to garnish

Instructions:

1. Place a non-stick skillet over medium-high heat. Add oil. When the oil is heated, add onions and sauté until onions are translucent.
2. Add quinoa and sauté for 3-4 minutes. Add water and salt and bring to the boil.
3. Lower heat, cover, and simmer until water is dried up. Remove from heat and keep covered for 15 minutes. Uncover, and fluff with a fork. Transfer to a serving bowl.
4. Add rest of the ingredients to the bowl and toss well.
5. To make dressing: Add all the ingredients to a small bowl and whisk well.
6. Pour dressing over salad and toss again.
7. Garnish with mint sprigs and serve.

Mushroom Alfredo

Prep: 20 min	Total: 45 min	Servings: 4

Ingredients:

- 16 ounces whole wheat spelt rotini or any other whole wheat pasta, cooked according to instructions on the package
- 1 pound mixed mushrooms, trimmed, sliced
- 4 tablespoons extra virgin olive oil
- 8 cloves garlic, minced
- 14 tablespoons almonds, sliced, divided
- 1 ½ cups almond milk, unsweetened
- 1 ½ teaspoons fine sea salt, divided
- 1 teaspoon freshly ground black pepper powder
- 4 tablespoons nutritional yeast
- ¼ cup fresh parsley, chopped

Instructions:

1. Place a large deep skillet or wok over medium-high heat. Add oil. When the oil is heated, add mushrooms and about a teaspoon salt. Sauté until brown.
2. Add garlic and sauté until fragrant.
3. Meanwhile, toast half the almonds and set aside. Add the remaining almonds to a blender and blend along with nutritional yeast and almond milk until smooth and creamy. Transfer this into the skillet.
4. Add pasta, salt, and pepper to the skillet and toss well.
5. Garnish with toasted almonds and parsley and serve.

Seafood Gazpacho

Prep: 20 min	Total: 35 min + chilling	Servings: 4

Ingredients:

- 1 pound bay scallops, rinsed, pat dried
- ½ pound shrimp, cooked, rinsed, pat dried
- 1 large yellow bell pepper, diced into ¼ inch pieces
- 1 medium onion, minced
- 2 medium tomatoes, deseeded, chopped
- 1 ⅓ cups cucumber, chopped
- 6 cloves garlic, peeled, pressed
- 4 tablespoons extra virgin olive oil
- 2 cans (4 ounces each) diced green chili
- 6 cups tomato juice
- Salt to taste
- Freshly cracked pepper to taste
- ½ cup lemon juice

- ½ cup fresh cilantro, chopped

Instructions:

1. Pour lemon juice over the scallops and set aside. If you don't like your scallops raw, then steam for just a minute and then marinate in lemon juice.
2. Add rest of the ingredients into a bowl and mix well. Set aside for a while.
3. Add scallops to it. Mix well and chill for at least an hour.
4. Serve chilled in soup bowls.

Chicken and Brown Rice Soup

Prep: 20 min	Total: 50 min	Servings: 6

Ingredients:

- 1 large chicken breast, cut into bite-sized pieces
- 3 stalks celery, chopped
- 1 large onion, chopped
- 5 medium carrots, peeled, chopped
- 1 ½ cups long grain brown rice
- 2 bay leaves
- 2 bunches collard greens, hard ribs and stems removed, thinly sliced
- 12 cups low-sodium chicken broth, divided
- 3 cups water
- Salt to taste
- Pepper powder to taste

Instructions:

1. Place a large pot over medium heat. Add ½ cup broth and bring to a boil. Add onions, carrots and celery and cook until the onions are translucent.
2. Add rest of the ingredients, except collard greens, and bring to the boil.
3. Lower heat, cover and cook until tender. Discard bay leaves.
4. Add collard greens, cook until wilted and serve immediately.

Halibut Salad

| Prep: 10 min | Total: 30 min | Servings: 3 |

Ingredients:

- 1 pound mixed salad greens, rinsed, pat dried
- 12 ounces halibut, steak or fillet
- 8 cloves garlic, peeled, pressed
- ⅔ cup fresh lemon juice
- 2 cups vegetable broth
- ⅓ cup fresh sage, minced or 2 tablespoons dried sage
- Salt to taste
- Pepper powder to taste
- 6 tablespoons extra virgin olive oil (optional)

Instructions:

1. Brush halibut steaks with lemon juice. Sprinkle salt and pepper.

2. Place a skillet over medium heat. Add broth, and halibut, cover, and cook until done.
3. Meanwhile, divide and place the salad greens over individual serving plates.
4. Place the cooked halibut over the greens.
5. Discard the broth in which the halibut is cooked. Add garlic, sage, and lemon juice to the skillet and heat for about 30 seconds.
6. Remove from heat and add olive oil if using. Drizzle over the salad. Season with salt and pepper and serve.

Chicken with Brussels sprouts and Mustard Sauce

Prep: 15 min	Total: 40 min	Servings: 2

Ingredients:

- 2 chicken breast halves (6 ounces each), skinless, boneless
- 3 teaspoons olive oil, divided
- 6 tablespoons fat-free chicken broth, divided
- 2 teaspoons butter, divided
- 2 tablespoons apple cider vinegar
- 2 teaspoons fresh flat leaf parsley, chopped
- 1 tablespoon whole grain Dijon mustard
- 6 ounces Brussels sprouts, trimmed, halved
- Salt to taste
- Pepper powder to taste

Instructions:

1. Place an ovenproof skillet over high heat. Add half the oil. When the oil is heated, add chicken.

Season with salt and pepper. Cook until brown on both sides.
2. Remove from heat and place the skillet in a preheated oven. Bake at 450° F for about 10 minutes or until tender.
3. Remove from the oven and keep warm.
4. Place the skillet back over medium-high heat. Add half the broth and apple cider vinegar and bring to the boil. Scrape the bottom of the skillet to remove the brown bits that are stuck at the bottom of the skillet.
5. Lower heat and simmer until the broth is thick. Add mustard, 1 teaspoon of butter and parsley and cook for a minute. Remove from heat.
6. Place a nonstick skillet over medium-high heat. Add remaining oil and butter. When the butter melts, add Brussels sprouts and sauté until it is light brown in color. Add salt and remaining broth. Stir.
7. Cover and cook until the Brussels sprouts are tender as well as crisp.

8. Place chicken on serving plates. Place Brussels sprouts alongside. Pour the thickened broth over the chicken and serve.

Chapter 5: Clean Eating Dinner Recipes

Grilled Teriyaki Pork Lettuce Wraps

Prep: 15 min	Total: 2hrs 30 min	Servings: 4

Ingredients:

- 1 pork tenderloin (about 2 pounds)
- 2 heads Boston Lettuce, separate leaves, rinse, pat dry
- ⅔ cup teriyaki sauce plus extra for serving
- 1 cup carrots, peeled, shredded
- 1 cup radish, shredded
- 1 cup cucumber, shredded
- 1 cup Napa cabbage, shredded
- 1 cup mixed fresh herbs of your choice, chopped

Instructions:

1. Place pork in a bowl and pour teriyaki sauce over it. Coat well and marinate for at least a couple of hours in the refrigerator.
2. Preheat a grill to medium-high. Carefully remove the pork from the bowl discarding the remaining marinade and place on the grill.
3. Grill until brown and tender. Turn pork frequently while it is grilling. If you think that the pork is getting brown and not getting cooked inside move the pork to a comparatively cooler part of the grill.
4. When done, place the pork on your cutting board. When cool enough to handle, slice it into thin strips.
5. Place lettuce leaves on individual serving plates.
6. Sprinkle vegetables over the leaves. Place pork strips on top. Sprinkle mixed herbs. Drizzle some teriyaki sauce over it and serve.

Sweet Potato Tofu Curry

| Prep: 20 min | Total: 45 min | Servings: 6 |

Ingredients:

- 2 large sweet potatoes, peeled, cubed
- 2 yellow onions, finely chopped
- 28 ounces tofu, drained, cubed
- 4 tablespoons coconut oil or any oil of your choice
- 1 tablespoon ginger paste
- 1 tablespoon garlic paste
- 4 bell peppers (use 2-3 colored ones), cut into 1-inch cubes
- 2 cups green beans, cut into 2-inch pieces
- 6 green chilies, ground
- 2 cans coconut milk
- 2 cans water
- 15-20 curry leaves
- 1 teaspoon ground cumin

- 2 teaspoons ground turmeric
- Salt to taste

To serve:
- 1 cup peanuts, roasted
- Cooked rice, as required
- ¼ teaspoon red chili flakes
- 4 green onions, thinly sliced

Instructions:

1. Place a large wok over medium heat. Add oil. When the oil is heated, add onions and sauté until translucent.
2. Add green chili paste, ginger paste, garlic paste, turmeric and ground cumin and sauté until light brown.
3. Add sweet potatoes and sauté for 4-5 minutes. Stir frequently. You can sprinkle water if you think the mixture is burning.
4. Add beans and bell peppers and sauté for 4-5 minutes.

5. Add tofu, coconut milk, water, salt, and tofu. Stir well.
6. Cover and cook until the sweet potatoes are tender. Taste and adjust the seasoning if necessary.
7. Place cooked brown rice on individual serving plates. Pour the curry over it. Sprinkle peanuts, chili flakes, and green onions on top and serve.

Creamy Risotto with Butternut Squash

| Prep: 15 min | Total: 45 min | Servings: 6 |

Ingredients:

- 2 cups raw cashews, soaked in water overnight, drained
- 5 cups butternut squash, peeled, deseeded, chopped
- 1 cup onion, chopped
- 6 cloves garlic, minced
- ½ cup fresh parsley, finely chopped
- 3 cups non-dairy milk like soy milk or almond milk
- 1 teaspoon fine sea salt
- 1 teaspoon ground cinnamon
- 2 packages (20 ounces each) frozen brown rice
- 1 ½ cups low sodium vegetable broth or more if required
- 4 tablespoons fresh sage, minced

- ½ teaspoon freshly ground black pepper
- Cooking spray

Instructions:

1. Place a large pot over medium heat. Add squash and cook until tender. Remove about 1 ½ cups of the squash and keep it aside.
2. Let the rest of the squash cook for another 10 minutes or until very soft. Drain and set aside
3. Meanwhile, blend together in a blender, cashew, softened squash, milk, cinnamon, and salt until smooth and creamy. Set aside.
4. Place a large skillet over medium heat. Spray with cooking spray. Add onions and garlic and sauté until light brown.
5. Add the cup of squash that was kept aside, brown rice and broth. Cook for 2-3 minutes stirring frequently. If you find it too dry, add some more broth.

6. Add creamy cashew mixture, sage and parsley. Stir and lower heat. Simmer until risotto of the desired thickness is achieved.
7. Remove from heat. Sprinkle black pepper powder and stir. Serve hot.

Baked Chicken with Peppers and Mushrooms

Prep: 15 min	Total: 50 min	Servings: 4

Ingredients:

- 1 ½ pound chicken breast or thigh, skinless, boneless
- 1 large bell pepper, chopped
- 1 cup mushrooms, chopped
- 1 onion, finely chopped
- 2 teaspoons coconut or avocado oil
- ¼ teaspoon Himalayan pink salt or to taste
- 1 teaspoon garlic, grated
- ½ cup low-fat mozzarella cheese, shredded
- Pepper powder to taste

Instructions:

1. Halve the chicken lengthwise (if using breasts) and place in a baking dish. Sprinkle salt, pepper, and garlic and mix well.

2. Cover and bake in a preheated oven at 425° F for about 20 minutes or until the chicken is tender.
3. Meanwhile, place a nonstick skillet over medium-low heat. Add oil. When the oil is heated, add onions and sauté until the onions are translucent. Add mushrooms and bell peppers and sauté for a few minutes until the vegetables are tender. Remove from heat.
4. Top the chicken with the cooked vegetables. Sprinkle cheese on top.
5. Broil for a few minutes until the cheese melts.
6. Serve with cooked quinoa or rice.

Thai Laksa Soup

Prep: 20 min	Total: 50 min	Servings: 6

Ingredients:

- 3 chicken breasts, sliced into chunks
- 1 pound prawns, peeled, tail on
- 12 stalks and leaves of Chinese broccoli (kai-lan), break into smaller pieces
- 2 carrots, peeled, chopped into matchsticks
- 2 zucchini, chopped into matchsticks
- 1 head broccoli, broken into florets
- 2 Lebanese cucumbers, chopped into matchsticks
- 10 tablespoons laksa paste
- 8 tablespoons fish sauce
- 4 cups chicken stock
- 3 cups full-fat coconut milk
- 2 teaspoons grated palm sugar (optional)
- 1 cup coconut cream
- 2 tablespoons coconut oil

- 2 tablespoons fresh cilantro, chopped
- 1 Thai chili, diced
- Salt to taste
- Juice of 2 limes

Instructions:

1. Place a large saucepan over medium heat. Add coconut oil. When the oil melts, add laksa paste and sauté for a couple of minutes. Stir constantly. Add more coconut oil if required.
2. Add stock, fish sauce, sugar, salt, and lime juice and bring to the boil.
3. Add chicken and cook for a couple of minutes. Remove chicken with a slotted spoon and place on your chopping board. When cool enough to handle, slice into thinner strips.
4. Lower heat and add coconut milk. Simmer for about 8-10 minutes.
5. Add carrots, kai lan, broccoli, and chicken. Let it cook for about 2 minutes. Add zucchini and prawns and cook for another 2 minutes. The prawns will curl as they cook.

6. Add coconut cream. Stir and remove from heat.
7. Ladle soup into individual soup bowls and serve.

Roast Turkey Breast with Chipotle Chili Sauce

| Prep: 15 min | Total: 30 min | Servings: 4 |

Ingredients:

For sauce:
- 1 large onion, minced
- 6 cloves garlic, minced
- 4 canned chipotle chilies, minced
- 4 tablespoons tomato paste
- 4 tablespoons Dijon mustard
- 2 cups chicken broth
- 2 tablespoons fresh oregano, chopped
- 4 tablespoons blackstrap molasses
- 1 tablespoon olive oil
- Salt to taste
- 1 turkey breast, roasted, sliced to serve

Instructions:

1. To make the sauce: Place a skillet over medium heat. Add oil. When oil is heated, add onions and sauté until onions are translucent. Add garlic and sauté until fragrant.
2. Add rest of the ingredients and simmer until thickened.
3. Serve roasted turkey with some sauce poured on it.

Shepherd's Pie

Prep: 15 min	Total: 1 hr. 30 min	Servings: 6-8

Ingredients:

- 3 large baking potatoes, peeled, diced
- ¾ cup low-fat milk
- 1 ½ pounds lean ground beef
- 3 medium onions, chopped
- 6 cloves garlic, minced
- 3 tablespoons whole wheat flour
- 6 cups frozen mixed vegetables
- 1 ½ cups low-sodium beef broth
- ¼ cup low-fat cheddar cheese, sliced
- Pepper powder to taste
- Salt to taste

Instructions:

1. Place the potatoes in a saucepan covered with water. Cook until the potatoes are soft. Drain and mash the potatoes.
2. Add milk to the mashed potatoes and mix well. Keep aside.
3. Place a skillet over medium heat. Add onion, garlic, and meat. Cook until the meat is browned.
4. Add vegetables and broth. Cook until thoroughly heated.
5. Transfer to a large baking dish. Spread the potato mixture over this.
6. Sprinkle cheese on top.
7. Bake in a preheated oven at 375° F degree for 25-30 minutes or until the cheese is lightly browned.

Grilled Pork Chops with Two-Melon Salsa

Prep: 15 min	Total: 30 min	Servings: 6

Ingredients:

For the salsa:
- 1 ½ cups honeydew melon
- 1 ½ cups seedless watermelon
- 1 ½ tablespoons jalapeño pepper, finely chopped
- 1 large sweet onion, finely chopped
- 2 tablespoons fresh lime juice
- 2 tablespoons fresh cilantro, chopped
- Salt to taste

For the pork chops:
- 6 pork chops (4 ounces each) center-cut pork chops, bones, trimmed of fat
- 3 teaspoons canola oil
- 1 teaspoon garlic powder
- 2 teaspoons chili powder

- Pepper powder to taste
- Salt to taste
- Cooking spray

Instructions:

1. To make salsa: Mix together all the ingredients for the salsa in a bowl. Cover and set aside.
2. To make the pork chops: Preheat a grill or cook in a grill pan over medium-high heat. Mix together oil, garlic powder, chili powder, pepper and salt in a bowl. Rub this mixture into the pork chops.
3. Grill the pork for 4 minutes per side or until done. Spray with cooking spray while cooking.
4. Serve pork chops with the melon salsa.

Beef Stew

Prep: 20 min	Total: 1 hr. 25 min	Servings: 4

Ingredients:

- ¾ pound lean beef stew meat
- 4 ounces mushrooms, sliced
- 1 medium sweet potato, peeled, rinsed, chopped into chunks
- 1 medium onion, chopped
- 1 stalk celery, chopped
- 1 large carrot, peeled, chopped into chunks
- 1 ½ tablespoons garlic, minced
- 1 tablespoon coconut oil
- 1 tablespoon butter
- 1 bay leaf
- 3 cups beef broth
- ½ teaspoon garlic powder
- 1 tablespoon arrowroot powder
- ½ tablespoon balsamic vinegar

- Salt to taste
- Pepper powder to taste

Instructions:

1. Place a large Dutch oven or saucepan over medium heat. Add coconut oil. When the oil melts, add onions and garlic and sauté until onions are translucent.
2. Sprinkle garlic powder, salt and pepper over meat. Coat it well.
3. Meanwhile, place a skillet over medium heat. Add ½ tablespoon butter. When the butter melts, add meat and cook on both the sides for about a minute each. Remove from the skillet and add it to the Dutch oven.
4. Add 2 cups of beef broth and lower the heat.
5. Add sweet potatoes, celery, carrots, and bay leaf and stir. Let it simmer.
6. Meanwhile, add remaining butter to the skillet. Add mushrooms and sauté until mushrooms are tender. Add vinegar and stir.

7. Add arrowroot powder to the remaining beef broth. Add this to the pan of mushrooms, stirring constantly until thick. Transfer to the Dutch oven. Mix well and simmer for about an hour or until the meat is cooked.
8. Ladle the stew into bowls and serve.

Caribbean Chicken Salad

Prep: 2 hrs. 10 minutes	Total: 2 hrs. 20 min	Servings: 2

Ingredients:

- 1 chicken breast half, skinless, boneless
- 1 medium onion, chopped
- 1 tomato, deseeded, chopped
- ½ pound mixed salad greens
- 1 teaspoon jalapeno pepper, minced
- A handful of cilantro, chopped
- ½ cup pineapple chunks, drained
- 2 tablespoons teriyaki marinade sauce
- 2 cups corn tortilla chips to serve, broken into large pieces

For dressing:

- 2 tablespoons Dijon mustard
- 2 teaspoons sugar

- 2 teaspoons apple cider
- ½ tablespoon olive oil
- 1 teaspoon lime juice
- 2 tablespoons honey

Instructions:

1. Place chicken breast in a bowl and pour teriyaki marinade sauce over it. Toss well and refrigerate for a minimum of 2 hours.
2. Mix together in a bowl, tomatoes, onion, jalapeño pepper, and cilantro and refrigerate until use.
3. For dressing: Mix together all the ingredients for dressing and whisk well. Cover and refrigerate until use.
4. Remove the marinated chicken from the refrigerator and grill on a preheated grill for about 6-8 minutes per side over high heat. Discard the marinade.
5. When done, remove from the grill. When cool enough to handle, cut the grilled chicken into strips.

6. To arrange salad: Place salad greens on a serving plate. Pour the tomato mixture over the greens. Layer with pineapple chunks.
7. Sprinkle tortilla chips over the pineapple layer. Place chicken strips on top.
8. Finally pour the dressing all over and serve.
9. You can also arrange, in a similar manner, on individual serving plates.

Cruciferous Peanut Butter Rice

| Prep: 20 min | Total: 50 min | Servings: 6 |

Ingredients:

- 2 cups long brown rice, rinsed, drained
- 1 large head red cabbage, chopped
- 1 large head cauliflower, chopped
- 2 packages firm tofu, cubed
- 4 cups water
- 4 tablespoons coconut oil, divided
- 2 teaspoons Himalayan pink salt, divided
- ½ cup green onions, chopped
- ½ cup fresh cilantro, chopped
- 2-3 tablespoons roasted peanuts

For peanut butter sauce:
- 1 cup peanut butter, unsalted
- 2 cups mango chunks, fresh or frozen
- 1 cup warm water

- 4 large cloves garlic, minced
- ½ cup soy sauce
- 2 inches ginger, peeled, minced

Instructions:

1. Place a pot over medium heat. Add water and rice and bring to the boil.
2. Cover and cook until the rice is tender.
3. Meanwhile, add all the ingredients of the peanut butter sauce into a blender and blend until smooth. Transfer to a bowl and set aside.
4. Place a large wok over medium heat. Add half the coconut oil. When the oil is melted, add cabbage and salt and sauté for a few minutes until the cabbage begins to char slightly.
5. Transfer onto a plate.
6. Pour the remaining oil in the wok. Add cauliflower and salt and sauté until tender.
7. Add the cooked rice and cabbage into the wok and stir. Remove from heat.
8. Add tofu and stir.

9. Sprinkle peanuts and green onions. Drizzle the peanut butter sauce and stir again.
10. Serve in individual plates either hot or warm.

Note: You can replace tofu with cooked chicken strips.

Farmers Market Kale Tacos

Prep: 25 min	Total: 45 min	Servings: 4

Ingredients:

- ½ a large bunch curly kale, discard hard stems and ribs, finely chopped
- ½ bunch radishes, sliced
- 1 large tomato, sliced
- 1 lime, sliced
- 4 teaspoons coconut oil or avocado oil
- ½ teaspoon pink Himalayan salt or to taste
- Salsa, as required
- Corn tortillas to serve, warm according to the instructions on the package
- 2 cloves garlic, minced
- 2 tablespoons fresh cilantro, chopped

For guacamole:

- 2 ripe avocados, peeled, pitted, mashed

- Juice of a lime or to taste
- 2 tablespoons fresh cilantro, finely chopped
- Salt to taste

Instructions:

1. To make guacamole: Mix together all the ingredients of guacamole in a bowl. Cover and set aside in the refrigerator until use.
2. Place a skillet, preferably a cast-iron skillet, over medium heat. Add 3 teaspoons of oil. When the oil is heated, add garlic and sauté until fragrant.
3. Add kale and sauté until the kale wilts. Add the remaining oil and salt and stir.
4. Remove from heat.
5. Place the tortillas on your work area. Divide and spread the cooked kale on it.
6. Place the radish and tomatoes slices on it. Spoon in some salsa. Sprinkle cilantro on top. Roll and serve with guacamole and lime slices.

Conclusion

I want to thank you for choosing this book. I hope that you loved and enjoyed reading it immensely.

The basic idea behind this book was to offer you a wife plethora of clean eating recipes; presenting a new meal plan that will help you lose weight in a healthy manner. The recipes included in this book will last you for 15 days without needing to repeat any of them. You can also find a variety of recipes online and in various clean eating books that can help you enhance your meal plan. Once you are experienced enough, you can also create your own recipes using your favorite ingredients.

Do remember to use fresh and organic ingredients while cooking. This not only increases the taste of your food but also makes it more nutrient-rich. Once again, I thank you for purchasing this book, and I hope you will love all the recipes included in it.

Good luck and happy cooking!

www.ingramcontent.com/pod-product-compliance
Lightning Source LLC
Chambersburg PA
CBHW070951080526
44587CB00015B/2258

www.ingramcontent.com/pod-product-compliance
Lightning Source LLC
Chambersburg PA
CBHW071630080526
44588CB00010B/1345

And they saw the God of Israel: and there was under His feet as it were paved work of sapphire stone, and as it were the body of heaven in His clearness.

Exodus 24: 10

Ask Him to fill you!
Ask Him to refill you!
He will give you power to overcome!

9 WAYS ~ TO BE FILLED WITH THE HOLY SPIRIT
1. Asking ~ Luke 11:13
2. When someone full of the Holy Ghost blows on you ~ John 20:21
3. When your in an atmosphere where He is descending ~ Matthew 3:16
4. By repenting and baptism ~ Acts 2:38
5. Laying on of hands ~ Acts 9:17, 18 Acts 19:6
6. Hearing the word of God ~ Acts 10:44-46
7. Praying while laying on hands ~ Acts 8:14-17
8. Praying ~ Acts 4:31, Luke 3:21
9. While speaking ~ Acts 11:15

Meet the Life Behind the Letter We Read!!!!!

CHAPTER TWENTY-SIX

The Ultimate Invitation

Jesus/Yeshua has so many blessings for us, and loves us so much. If you have not accepted Him into your heart, please make the decision to do it now.

He, alone, can cleanse you. Just come to Him as you are. He will accept you, just like He accepted me. He will cleanse you, just like He cleansed me.

Tell Him you believe He's the Son of God, and that you believe He died and arose for your sins. Ask Him to come into your heart, cleanse you, and fill you with His precious Holy Spirit.

The best thing that ever happened to me was Jesus saving me, filling me with His Holy Spirit, and teaching me how to enter into His Presence.

The Holy Spirit is so kind, very loving, and the only Person who can help you.

He desires to engulf you!

He longs to fellowship with you!

He will teach you what is freely given to you!

The Holy Spirit will reveal your purpose!

That Friday, after I repented, the Holy Spirit spoke to me, saying, *"I allowed this to happen to you so you would let My people know that accidents happen and attached to accidents is fear, not faith. Fear, at times, has made it impossible for a person to repent. Yes, I allow things to happen, just like I allow you to choose what you do with your life. If your life had ended with that fall, you wouldn't have been with Me."*

God told me to call over a relative and lay my hands on her, then pray for her protection. She and her husband came over, and I did as the Holy Spirit commanded.

They went to a club that night, and there was an altercation. A man stood three feet in front of her, pointing his pistol in her face. She said she heard the Holy Spirit whisper, *"Jump!"* So, she jumped, and he fired. She said the bullet was moving in slow motion, and when it got to her nose it fell to the ground.

She said the Holy Spirit whispered a second time, *"Jump!"* and he fired again. That bullet also moved in slow motion, got to her face and again fell to the ground.

Her husband came around the corner, shouting, "Hey! That's my wife!"

The man turned, aiming the gun at her husband, and she shouted, "Run!" as she ran. Her husband ran, but was shot in the back. As he fell, the man stood over him pointing the gun to his head. At that point, he started begging God, "Please don't let him kill me!"

Every time the man attempted to fire the gun, it jammed! *IT'S SUPERNATURAL!!!*

her life to God, saying, "We can do it right here. No one will have to know." She still refused.

Later that evening, there was an accident and she was seriously injured. The doctors said she was getting better and everyone was happy.

After 1 a.m. one morning, I started sliding off the bed, down to my knees, and a vision appeared. I saw the lady going through a tunnel of fire screaming, "It's real! It's real! Oh, my God, it's real!" And then she died.

I called her best friend, telling her she just died, and she responded, "No, we just left her and everything looks good."

I said, "No, sweetheart, I just saw her and she's gone."

The best friend got in touch with the family and they told her the woman had just passed.

Two years after I gave my heart to the Lord, I got mad at God because my son got in trouble. I told God I didn't want to serve Him anymore. I felt like he hadn't protected him, because I knew that nothing happens unless He allows it! I was under the impression that if I served God, He wouldn't let anything happen to my children.

Two weeks had gone by after I made the decision not to serve Him anymore. I refused to read, study, pray, or go to service.

The Holy Spirit spoke to me one Wednesday saying, **"Go to Bible Study. Someone is expecting you to be there!"**

I said no.

That Thursday, I fell and hit my head on concrete and was unconscious.

CHAPTER TWENTY-FIVE

It's Real! It's Real!

There are so many things the Holy Spirit reveals in the Presence of Jesus. We can't change people, but the Presence of Jesus/Yeshua can. Our duty is to get them to Jesus, and He will give them the power to overcome. Some things He tells us to do, we may not understand or know the purpose of, but we need to do it because someone's life may depend upon it.

Once the Holy Spirit asked me to talk to a lady about accepting Him. I did, but she refused. I went to her for six days, and she still refused, but promised me she would come to church that Sunday.

On Sunday, she came to Church, but didn't give her life to the Lord. I met her after service and begged her to give

Though Jesus, by the Holy Spirit, to the Father. In the Holy Spirit's ministry, He has laws, one of the laws is life.

> The law of the Spirit of life has made me free from the law of sin and death.
>
> Romans 8:2

Attached to Him is life and liveliness. There's freedom in His ministry! You are free to live in the Spirit and enjoy Him! He makes you a competent minister.

> He has made us competent ministers of a new covenant — not of the letter but of the Spirit; for the letter kills but the Spirit gives life.
>
> 2 Corinthians 3:6

You will not only know the scriptures (letter) you will experience the life of the author of the letter. In His ministry, the glory manifests. His Glory, at times, will be seen and felt by others around you, and looked upon by you. His Presence will rest upon you in exuberance, giving you the ability to share His Presence with others. His ministry brings righteousness, and transformation consistently.

Holy Spirit's ministry also consists of the great. Greater glory that will last, in His law of great. There is a such thing as joy and peace, but in His ministry there's great joy, great peace, great insight, great signs and wonders, great goodness, great miracles, great favor, great honor, great revelations, great reward, great wealth, great power, great faith, great abundance, great grace as well as great persecution. Ask Him to allow you to become one with Him in ministry.

Peter had a ministry. The ministry he was entrusted with allowed him to speak the word boldly, and as he spoke the Holy Ghost fell upon the hearers. Peter was so full of the Holy Ghost, in Acts 5:15 many laid the sick in the streets, so that at least his shadow might fall on some of them as he passed by.

Romans 12:3-8 lets us know that there are different types of ministries, but all types are in the Holy Ghost, if He's in charge! Jesus/Yeshua has a ministry, Luke 3: 23 reads, "Now Jesus himself was about thirty years old when he began his ministry." Jesus's ministry was founded on better promises, a ministry of reconciliation.

The Holy Spirit has a ministry. His ministry picked up where Jesus's left off. This is one of the reasons Jesus said, "I will send you another like Me."

When the Holy Spirit asked me if I would like to be a part of His ministry, He began teaching me what His ministry consists of. When we become a part of His ministry. the first thing you will experience is His fire. You will have a Holy passion stirred in you that's unquenchable! This process causes you to melt within, so that He may merge you and allow you to become one with Him in ministry.

One of the signs that you're there is the capacity of love you have for others, no matter what state or condition they're in. He is your only qualification for His ministry, and what allows Him to qualify you is your love for Yeshua and if you are surrendered to Him.

He works according to His will and will not promote our agenda. No one has to vote concerning Him; He alone is the majority vote. The Holy Spirit is our only access to the Father — we can't go around Him.

> For through him we both have access by one Spirit to the father.
>
> Ephesians 2:18

CHAPTER TWENTY-FOUR

Ministry of the Holy Spirit

> [7] Now if the ministry that brought death, which was engraved in letters on stone, came with glory, so that the Israelites could not look steadily at the face of Moses because of its glory, fading though it was, [8] will not the ministry of the Spirit be even more glorious? [9] If the ministry that condemns men is glorious, how much more glorious is the ministry that brings righteousness! [10] For what was glorious has no glory in comparison with the surpassing glory. [11] And if what was fading away came with glory, how much greater is the glory of that which lasts!
>
> 2 Corinthians 3:7 -11

The largest ministry written in the Bible given to man is that of Moses. Moses led over two million people forty years or more. Paul also had a large ministry, he was appointed by Jesus/Yeshua to reach the Gentiles in Acts 26: 15 -18.

He said, *"You are my witness on the earth. Don't speak for Me, allow Me to speak through you! You are one of My witnesses on the earth."* He said this because I asked what He wanted me to do.

He then said, *"Walk with Rufus in Me. He will change doctrines and Triumph will become a Spirit-filled church. I am pleased with how he has managed the church affairs. Share with him what I am saying to you, and what you are experiencing in Me. Now go back!"*

I had a knowing. It was 10:49 p.m. As Jesus/Yeshua was leaving, I said, "Wait! Wait! Don't go! I want to be with You."

He then said, *"Do you enjoy My Presence?"*

I said, "Yes."

I was about to ask Him about the boxes, and He said, *"Every time you come into my Presence a withdrawal is being made to you. Now go back and write these things down."*

I said, "Will you remind me?"

He said, *"Yes! Now go back!"*

I got up, walked in my room, and it was 10:48.

don't start releasing what God is giving you, His power will become violent upon you."

One night as I got in God's presence, suddenly a man appeared aglow. As I lay on what appeared to be a basement floor, He picked my limp body up, carrying me up some stairs. As we reached the top of the stairs, He stood me on my feet in what appeared to be a large storage/inventory room. I looked around the room, and there were huge white boxes as far as my eyes could see. The boxes had names on them.

When I approached the middle of the room, I saw my name. I had a knowing, there were contents in the boxes that were tied to our lives on earth. I opened the box with my name on it, and there were white sheets of paper, a pen and a gold lock inside. I put the lid back on my box, looked up, and I saw Shonta Coney's name.

As we moved into another room, it looked like a massive banquet hall. A light began moving towards us, and Jesus began to speak. I asked Him to do something for my son, and He said, *"It is done!"*

Seven things I asked him, pertaining to my son, and His response was the same each time, *"It is done!"*

I asked Him, "How did I get here?"

The Holy Spirit standing with me said, *"I brought you here!"*

At that time I was studying on heaven, so I asked Him, "How will we look in our heavenly bodies?"

He responded, *"Look at the framed picture in your room. That's how you would look in glory."*

Once in service, Jesus appeared standing alongside the pastor. As the people came down the aisle, He was pouring a gold substance upon them. One lady He pulled back three times, pouring that gold substance upon her.

Once a lady came to me after service and said, "You were laid out on the altar today."

I said, "No, I wasn't."

She said, "Yes, you were. I had my eyes closed, but I saw you."

That bothered me because I didn't even go to the altar that Sunday. The next Sunday, as I stood in the pew with my hands lifted as we worshipped, I saw myself come out of myself and go lay on the altar. Then I came back into my body.

The first four years of my walk with Jesus, His Presence would be so strong on me, but I didn't want anyone to know. He would speak to me something to share, but I wouldn't say it.

When His power would fall on me, it would be kind of forceful. I would see myself turning flips, but naturally standing upright.

The first year Brother Keith would have to carry me out of service — EVERY SERVICE! It started embarrassing me. A lady came up to me after a service and said, "If you

CHAPTER TWENTY-THREE

A Seer Sees What I'm Doing

One evening as I lay in the presence of God, waiting to hear from Him, I was transported to heaven. I was accompanied by two angels on each side as we walked down what looked like a huge hall with flooring in the shape of square stones, I asked the angel, "Where are we going?" One put his finger up to his mouth as if he were telling me to be quiet.

As we went into a room, Jesus/Yeshua was sitting at this huge table. He reached behind Him and came back with a huge book. The book flapped open, and the pages were blank. Jesus/Yeshua pointed to the book and it started writing my name incursive.

Then He reached behind him again, came up with a crown and placed it on my head, saying, **"He that win souls is wise."**

He then said, "The reason I stopped here is because when I was walking to this door, he said 'No! No! Don't go over there. I can't go in there.' So, if you would, please let me come in just for a moment to get some relief."

I let him come in, ministered to him for hours, and prayed for him. He gave his life to Jesus, and the tormentor left him!

walked over to her bed and started praying, then she said, "She's gone."

Then, she said, "Tina, I see Jesus. He's so beautiful." She started waving her hand, saying, "There's a rainbow behind Him. Wow! Pat is with Him! Look at his clothes!"

Then she was lost in ecstasy, and she started worshipping God. So I just joined in. After she finished, we talked about it. I didn't see them, but she did. Sometimes, Jesus will manifest in our midst and we may not see Him, but someone else may.

We had a prayer meeting at 5 a.m. one morning. We were all prostrated on the floor in silence in His Presence. My friend Tammy saw Jesus walking around while we were laid out. Two others saw Him, but I didn't. What I saw was something like a sheet hovering over us, as if it were silk.

Tammy and I were working one day, and a man walked up to the door and it scared the clients. I went out to talk with him and he said, "Ma'am, I'm sorry. I just made it home from the state hospital. I checked myself in there because the devil kept telling me to kill different people, and I didn't want to hurt nobody."

In the hospital, he didn't show up, but as soon as I returned home, I could see him again. He's been following me around since last night. He proceeded to say, "I'm not trying to make you afraid. but can you see him? He's standing beside me."

I said, "No, sir, but I believe *you* see him."

I said, "No one will be here with you to get you to the bathroom when I'm working."

She said, "Take me by Towie's until you get off work and come to get me. If you need to go back to work, Jeff can take me to the bathroom or I'll wait 'til you get back."

I agreed, and that night I told the Holy Spirit, "Don't let my grandma die in my home, 'cause I will never live there again if she does."

After I got her into bed one night, the Holy Spirit said, **"Don't give her the medicine tonight."**

After I went to sleep, He said, **"She's falling!"** So, I got up and walked to the door, but everything appeared normal.

That next morning while cooking her breakfast, He said, **"Don't give her the medicine."**

I went to feed her, and she said, "Tina, I fell last night, and was calling you, but you didn't hear me."

I said, "Why didn't you ring the bell?"

She ate and it was time for me to get her to her appointment. As she stood up, she couldn't walk. I called my mom, and she said, "Get her to the doctor right away. I'll call Bug, and be on my way."

I picked my grandma up, put her in the car, and got her to the doctor. She'd had a stroke! The doctor said if I had given her the medicine, she would've instantly died!

Damage was done to her heart, so they put her in the heart center, where you can only visit at certain times. During visitation, she said, "Ask them to let you stay with me. I don't want to be by myself, I keep seeing things." She said, "It's a person that keeps coming in the room to torment me. She looks like a nurse, but something keeps stopping the nurse from touching me."

She and I prayed and they let me stay. That night, she said, "Tina, there's the nurse," but I didn't see the nurse. I

He replied, *"Don't be sad. She will be changed! I will allow you some time to grieve, so that you can strengthen the others. Don't pray for her, for she will be changed! She will be with Me!"*

Oh my God! This was the first time I'd heard Him ask me not to pray! I was confused and grieved. *Why would You ask me to not pray? I thought Your will was that I pray for people to stay alive.* He didn't say another word.

I went from having an awesome experience, to a moment of dread. My grandma wasn't sick! *How am I going to share this with the others?* It hurt to think about it! *How will I get the words out of my mouth?*

We have a large family. My grandma had five children, and 75 grands, including great- and great-greatgrands who she fed every Sunday, along with their husbands and wives. She bought us all gifts weekly, sometimes two or three, depending on how many days in the week you visited. If you only came on Sundays, then you only received a Sunday gift. She told all of us secretly that we were her favorite!

I called Amanda, my Auntie Sharon, and my pastor, sharing with them what the Holy Ghost spoke to me.

On April 14, 2007, my mom called and said she was taking my grandma to her annual doctor's appointment. My mom called me later and said they gave my grandma four months to live.

When she got down sick, we took turns having her stay with each of us. In October, during my week, she asked, "Tina, what did Jesus say about me? Am I going to die?"

I said, "He's going to take care of you."

She said, "I want to stay with you, Bug is never home, Shelia needs to be with her husband, and Dick stays too far away."

CHAPTER TWENTY-TWO

She Will Be Changed

In January 2007, my grandpa died. We spent a lot of time with my grandma, who was happy and content just being around us. I went over salvation with my grandma back in 2002, and she started going to Church with me. She even followed Amanda and I to some of the deliverance services. My grandma, Amanda and I made a pact, saying if something happened to either one of us, we'd pray until there was a change.

On April 2, 2007, after worship, I was having an awesome experience in God! His Presence was so pleasant; all I could do was bow.

Then Jesus spoke, *"I'm bringing your grandmother home."*

I responded, "Huh?"

He said, *"I'm bringing your grandmother home with Me."*

I cried, "Please don't take my grandma! Please, I'll do anything. Please don't take her. I need her."

Mother shared another experience with me. She said one night while she was watching a show called *Ironside*, the television screen was suddenly filled with static. At that point, a lady walked into her room wearing a white gown on with pink roses on it. The lady told her not to spend another night there, and she turned and walked away. But then she turned back, pointed her index finger at my mom and told her, "Not another night." Then the *Ironside* program came back on the TV.

After she shared this experience, I thought about it, but still didn't want to know what it meant.

So, after prayer one night, the Holy Spirit began to speak, **"Your grandmother asked me to send an angel to protect your mother. She also asked me to send one to protect her also. She asked that I give you an interpretation of the angel you saw. The angel you saw is the angel assigned to your family."**

After arriving at the hospital, I asked my grandmother, "Why did you ask God to reveal to me the meaning of the lady?"

She said, "Because I knew He would. Now, what did He say?"

Later my cousin brought me a picture of my grandma, Big Mama, wearing a white dress with pink roses on it.

After getting home, I was sitting in my den and felt someone walk behind me. As I turned, I saw it was the lady again.

I told my mom about it, and she shared something with me something that happened to her when I was about five years old. My mom was born and raised in Baertown, where everyone watched out for each other. She proceeded to tell me her story.

She said she needed a ride from work, and called three of her Baertown friends to come and pick her up. Afterwards, they picked the three of us children up, too, dropping us off at home.

When they got to our apartment, they got very quiet. They brought the three of us in and put us on the couch. Then, they brought the bags in, and headed back to their car without saying a word. Mom said they would normally tell jokes and talk, but they didn't this time. She followed them out the door, asking them what was wrong. No one responded and they just got in their car and drove off.

The next day she said she saw them and asked them why were they acting like that. They told her that a lady was standing in her apartment when they came in and that she told them to sit us down, then bring in the bags and leave quietly. She told them there wasn't anyone in her apartment.

They insisted someone was there and even described what she was wearing: a white dress with pink roses on it. My mom told them again, there was no one in her apartment. She said, "If a lady was there, where was she standing that I didn't see her? They told her the lady was standing beside the couch when they came in and then she moved to stand behind my mom when she was at the door. They also said the woman looked mean. Mother told them she didn't believe them, and asked if they were on drugs.

Paw-Paw was the one sick, but I had a knowing, that the lady's visit had something to do with Maw-Maw Helen.

I looked at the clock, and saw it was a little after 5 a. m. It seemed as if dew had rested in the house.

Around 6 a.m. I called my mom and told her what happened, expecting her to help me understand, but she said she couldn't. I left about 6:30 a.m. to get my boys off to school.

As my mom came to get my paw-paw dressed for his doctor's appointment, I called Tammy and shared the experience with her, hoping she could help me to understand it. My mom did take my paw-paw to the doctor, and the doctors admitted him to the hospital.

About 10 a. m., my cousin called, and said she'd called an ambulance for Maw-Maw, because she thought she was having a heart attack.

Tammy picked me up, and we went to see what was happening. My sister was with Maw-Maw, speaking in her heavenly tongue language, while the paramedics worked on her. After arriving at the hospital, my cousin, who was older than me, came. So, I shared the experience with her. She said it sounded like I was describing a gown she saw on a picture of Big Mama.

My grandma stayed in the hospital for about two weeks, with Paw-Paw being across the hall. But he didn't know she was there.

I shared the experience with my grandma and she said that it sounded like I was describing her grandmother. I told her that it might have been the appearance of her grandmother, but it was an angel. This was different for me, because I never was able to determine gender. She told me to ask the Lord what it meant, and I told her I didn't want to know.

CHAPTER TWENTY-ONE

Who is that Lady?

My grandpa got sick in October 2006, and my grandma wasn't able to take care of him alone, so we all took turns helping. It was my night to stay with them and relieve the other two that were there.

I arrived at their home a few minutes before midnight, and decided I would worship instead of reading. I worshiped until around 4 a. m. As I lay there in silence with my hands lifted to God, the atmosphere began to change. The room got foggy as His Presence rested there.

As I lay there in awe, a lady walked up the hall and into the living room. She was wearing a dress with small pink roses on it that stood out to me. She had long hair and an intense look on her face. It was as if I knew her, but I'd never seen her before.

She bent down over me, looked me in my face, turned around and started walking towards the back room. She motioned for me to follow her. I got up, went to the hall, but she was gone!

thing in this house was supposed to have blown up! *IT'S SUPERNATURAL!*

Vet needed new kidneys. We prayed and prayed, but the results were the same. One particular day, before she had to go start dialysis, I got in His Presence and had been there for hours.

I called Vet and told her to come over before her appointment. After she arrived, the Holy Spirit instructed me to lay hands on her. After laying hands, I said new kidneys come into her body!

She went to her appointment they examined her before putting her on dialysis. The doctor told her she had new kidneys! Vet is walking around with kidneys from heaven in her body! *IT'S SUPERNATURAL!*

I went to pray for a lady that was locked in her home and on her last breath. When I arrived, the paramedics were there and couldn't get a pulse. The Holy Spirit said, ***"Lay on top of her, take your tears, and rub them on her back. Do it three times."*** I did, but by the second time, nothing happened.

I looked at the paramedic and he pointed to his watch, showing the other paramedic how long it had been. As I stood by the bathroom door watching them, he started to write on his notepad. I grabbed his arm and asked, "What are you doing?" He started to explain how a person can't be deprived of oxygen for that long.

I interrupted and said, "I understand, but she's not going to die. Check her again!"

He did it about four times, but nothing had changed.

I laid on the lady for the third time and wiped my tears on her, speaking in my heavenly language. All of a sudden her body started vibrating, then she started screaming and moving her hands as if she was fighting.

Later, I went to visit her and this is what she said, "Tina, I had left here. I couldn't see or hear anything. Then, all at once I heard your voice, but you were speaking in another language. As I heard that language, everything inside me started moving. It was like my body was being shocked."

That lady is alive and well! *IT'S SUPERNATURAL!*

Years ago, my fireplace caught fire. I tried to put the fire out, but it blazed up onto the walls and ceiling. A fireman came and put the fire out. He said to me, "You are lucky! Your gas line is full of gas! You, everybody and every-

When she saw what was happening, she ran to get the others. While she was gone, I slipped out the side door. *IT'S SUPERNATURAL!*

I had been in prayer for a man who had cancer in the fourth stage. He's now cancer free! Totally healed by the power of God no medicine! *IT'S SUPERNATURAL!*

For a season, the Holy Spirit had me laying hands on women that wanted children. Five different ladies got pregnant and delivered their babies. A few years later, the Holy Spirit told me to go to a school and walk around on campus. I did. After a while He said, **"Run!**

I started running, and as I ran a vision appeared. I saw a child falling backwards. The vision disappeared as I came to some double doors. When I opened the doors, there stood a child, vomiting.

As she began to fall, I caught her. Her body went limp in my arms and I started speaking in my heavenly language. The child came-to and squeezed me around my neck, then I handed her to the teacher.

I found out the next day she was one of the babies born as of the result of the laying on of hands. *IT'S SUPERNATURAL!*

I had a meeting one Monday. The person I was meeting with had inherited millions of dollars and wanted to do something for me. I'd been praying with this person for years, about some things God would do for them, and God did it!

After the meeting, the person said they wanted to give me $1.2 million. I got so excited! After our conversation, we decided the time we could meet the next day so they could bring me the check.

That night I couldn't sleep.

That next day, after prayer and worship the Holy Spirit said, **"Don't accept it."**

We met, and the person took out the check and gave it to me. I gave it back and told them why I couldn't take it. *IT'S SUPERNATURAL!*

The Lord kept showing me a room number. That next week, I had to go to a medical center to deliver some documents. As I walked down the hall, I saw that number on a door. The next day, I went back and a lady was outside the door. I asked if I could go in and she said, "Yes, but the woman in that room has been in a coma for years."

I walked over to the bed, very unsure of what He wanted me to do. I began talking telling her I wanted to pray for her. After prayer, the lady woke up, trying to talk very quietly, then she got louder. She was so loud that the lady I'd talked to outside came in.

Instantly the Holy Spirit said, ***"No!"***

After I turned down the car, my husband was mad at me for two weeks. *IT'S SUPERNATURAL!*

Scherry and I went to a rehab to pray for someone who'd had a stroke. When we finished praying for the lady, another lady followed us out, asking if we could pray for her, too. She'd been deaf in one ear for years.

Scherry anointed her with oil, and I stuck my index finger in the oil and then stuck it in her ear and commanded it to open. I whispered in that ear, asking her to repeat after me, and she did! God opened up her ear!

Later, she ran into a lady and was telling her about it, and the lady knew me. She called and let me talk to the other lady, and not only did God unstop her ear, he healed the rest of her body from an illness she'd had for twenty years! *IT'S SUPERNATURAL!*

The Holy Spirit said that someone would give me $4,000 and told me what to do with it. I was at the gas station pumping gas, when a car pulled up. The person inside said, "I've been looking for you," and handed me a check for $3,000.

I left there and went to the supermarket. A lady walked out the store as I was entering and said, "Wait! The Lord told me I would see you today and to give you $1,000. He said you would know what to do with it." *IT'S SUPERNATURAL!*

I said, "Oh no, you're not!" I jumped on top of his truck and started praying. The color came back to his face, and his breathing regulated. God healed him!

Later that day, my husband and I were driving and saw the same truck parked on the side of the street. I made my husband get out and look for the man, because we didn't see him in the truck. My husband was about to walk to a house to see if someone had seen him, when we spotted him behind the house mowing the yard. *IT'S SUPERNATURAL!*

A friend who lives out of state called me, saying a friend of his only had a few days to live. His friend needed a liver. I asked him if he believed God could heal his friend, and he said yes.

I said, "New Liver come into his body in Jesus' name!" Then said, "Okay, brother, have a nice day." Then, I got off the phone.

His friend received that new liver and is alive today! *IT'S SUPERNATURAL!*

The Holy Spirit sent me to a rich guy to give him a message. He got my phone number and later called me to come by his place. My husband and I went there, and he said, "I have something for you." He threw me some keys and told me to walk outside. As we went outside, he said, "I special ordered a Mercedes, it cost me $90,000 but I don't like it and I want to give it to you."

The next day we sent my mom back to check on the guy, and he told her he was dead and Jesus told him to "Get up!" *IT'S SUPERNATURAL!*

The Holy Spirit instructed me to go to my son's grandmother's house and take my prayer shawl. I was to walk up to my oldest son, who moved in with his grandmother, then walk seven steps backwards and throw the prayer shawl up in the air. When I did this, the prayer shawl came down and fell on my son's head, clinging to his face. I fell to the ground, and Vet who tried to help me get up, fell also.

The next morning around 5 a.m., my son's grandmother called, saying, "Get to the hospital." She'd found my son pinned under the car, with the car sitting on his head.

I got to the hospital after they'd run the tests on him and he had no broken bones, cuts or abrasions! *IT'S SUPERNATURAL!*

Scherry and I were on the phone one morning, and the Holy Spirit said, ***"Go to the mailbox!"***

I walked to the mailbox, as I stood there an oversized truck came down the road. It was swerving, and was about to hit me. The truck stopped beside me, and the guy slumped over in the seat, grasping for air. I asked, "What's wrong?"

He said, "I can't breathe. I'm having another heart attack."

I slowly opened my eyes and saw we were in the middle of the highway with no deer in front of us. I called Jackie and Roneek's names, telling them we were safe.

Roneek asked, "What happened? Where did they go?"

We heard a thump behind the truck, looked back there, and all three of them were standing behind the truck. We went right through them, as if the truck were invisible.

Roneek said, "What do we do?"
I shouted, "Drive! *IT'S SUPERNATURAL!*"

Amanda and I were instructed to go pray for someone the doctors had given up on. When we got there, we asked his relatives if we could go in and pray. One of them replied, "Yes, but it won't do no good. He's on life support and they're going to take him off soon."

We went over to the bed, and my sister began speaking in her heavenly language. I said, "Father, I thank you that you hear me and I know you always hear me, but I'm saying this for their sake" (pointing at the relatives). Then I called the person's name and told them to get up "in Jesus' name, Amen."

We turned to say goodbye to the relatives, then the alarm on the life support machine started going off. The patient's eyes opened, and his hands started reaching for my sister and me.

The staff ran in and moved us out of the hospital room, so Amanda and I left. We left there looking for sick people so that we could pray for them.

CHAPTER TWENTY

Kidneys From Heaven

After learning how to worship, the Presence of God started resting upon on me daily. The more I worshipped, the stronger His Presence became. The longer I worshipped, the longer His Presence rested, and the more supernatural things started happening in my life.

I was traveling on the highway with my friend Jackie and baby sister Roneek. Roneek was driving my truck, while I sat on the passenger side and Jackie sat in the back. As we topped a hill on a one-way road going 70 mph, there were three deers with antlers standing in the middle of highway.

On one side of the highway was about a forty-foot drop, and on the other side maybe a twenty-five foot drop. Roneek screamed, took both her hands off the wheel, and covered her eyes. Jackie got down on the floor of the backseat, and I closed my eyes, threw my hands up and shouted "Jesus!"

The truck stopped, and my sister was screaming, "We're dead! We're dead!"

After looking, I didn't see anything on my face. So I looked again. As I turned to walk away, He said, *"I created the outside to see in, and the inside to see out."* When I would see Him in others, or sense His Presence, it provoked me to praise.

This was happening everywhere I went. Sometimes, I would be driving, and then pull over just to praise Him. When people would stand up and talk in service, He would appear in their countenance."

This really helped me at times when He was giving someone a message to release. God's holiness is His Glory revealed inside of us. God's Glory is His holiness revealed on the outside of us.

Feeling so overwhelmed with supernatural exuberance, I asked Him to show others.

He said, *"I have. You are free to share. You are free in Me."*

I was excited often about what was occurring, and wanted others to experience Him. Nothing else mattered.

Then He said, *"I'm delivering you from shock. You shouldn't be surprised by what you see in Me!"*

I was so excited about Him, and enjoyed being in His Presence. I had no desire for anything else. He's a great teacher and friend.

The longest conversation I've had with Him was when He revealed Jesus/Yeshua to me in the Old Testament. I believe He was more excited to share it with me than I was hearing it revealed.

In His Presence, He reveals so many things. Once, I saw feathers gliding past me! This alone compels me to enjoy my freedom walk in Him, IN HIS PRESENCE!

> I have given them the glory that you have given me that they may be one even as we are one: Jesus was praying for all believers.
>
> John 17:22

My question to the Holy Ghost was, "What glory did He give us believers?"

He said, **"Me!"**

The Holy Spirit is the Spirit of Glory!

If you are insulted because of the name of Christ, you are blessed, for the Spirit of Glory and of God rests on you."

> I consider that our present suffering is not worth comparing with the glory that will be revealed in us.
>
> Romans 8:18

The Holy Spirit is the Spirit of Glory in us!

After The Holy Spirit, released me to share the image He had given me. I started seeing Him in other people's countenances — people that I came into physical contact with, and different ministers on television.

One night around 11:30, I was watching a minister on television and the Holy Ghost was resting in His countenance. This shocked me! I jumped up and started shouting, praising God.

I ran into the other room and got Shenitha, and then she and I watched the minister as the fire of God fell on us and we danced and praised God 'til after 4 a.m. Everybody in the house was up.

I spent the next two weeks asking God what was happening to me. He never responded. One day, He said, **"Look in the mirror."**

The prophet said she had seen that same image, but wanted me to say out of my mouth who the image was.

After having that experience in 2012, the Holy Spirit said for me to share the image in Bible Study one night. He said, **"I have released you to share what I asked you to draw."**

"I responded, "Are You sure?"

He replied, **"I have released you to do so. You're always safe when you do as I say, and say what I've said."**

He let me know the underlying factor of why I chose not to share; it was because I didn't feel it was safe. I didn't want to put people in a position to speak against Him. He said I was trying to defend Him, and He didn't need me defending Him. I should just do as He says.

Once, a pastor said He didn't have a body, and as soon as he said it, He manifested. I was grieved for months because of what the pastor said. Then, finally I went to him and told him how grieved I was and why. He said, "No I didn't mean it like that. If you see Him as an 'it,' you will treat Him like a thing. If you view Him as a power, you will try and use Him. He's a Person with a personality. When you see Him as a Person, the most important Person on earth, you'll respect Him. Your body you, looks like your soul you, your body and soul you looks like your spirit you.

So it is with God. This is one of the reasons Jesus was able to make the bold statement, 'When you have seen Me, you've seen the Father. I and the Father are one.' God will never create something, or someone better than who He is.

the tricycle, because I was holding on to them as they drove, but they were invisible.

All at once, the person turned around, and I could see their eyes and some of their form. I then flipped backwards off the unusual tricycle. As I flipped, the person came up under me, grabbed me, stood me upright, leaving me face to face with Him. He then started blowing in my face, and these words formed in a diagonal manner

    I
     N
      T
       I
        M
         A
          C
           Y

then went into my body. I then began to flip backwards again. As I came to myself, I was sitting on my prayer room floor. The person I saw was the same image standing behind me that appeared in a vision in front of me, the Holy Spirit told me to draw.

I've been seeing this image for seventeen years now. This image is written in every notebook I have, even drawn on poster boards in my home. For years I've not wanted to share this image and only showed it to someone once before 2012.

Prior to 2012, the Holy Spirit told me to share the image with an out of town prophet who visited me. I was hesitant, but did what He asked. As I showed the image to the prophet, she began flipping under the power of God, and afterwards asked me who it was. I told her I couldn't say. She pleaded with me, but I just couldn't talk about the image.

I said, "I have on heels!" Took the heels off and went into the kitchen to help serve. While serving, I saw the person who had invited me peeking around a column at me. I caught them doing that three times.

A man came in the kitchen, touched me on my shoulder, then walked off. I started saying to myself, *There's something wrong with these people! I'm going to finish serving and leave.*

I finished and went out and got in my truck. I looked in the mirror, checking to see if I had something in my nose or on my face, but nothing was there. That next day, the person who invited me called me at work and said, "I was disappointed you didn't show up. I wanted you to speak."

I said, "I was there, but everybody was acting so weird, even you, so I helped serve the food, then I left."

The person asked, "That was you in the kitchen? We were trying to figure out if you were a real person! That was my relative who touched you on your shoulder. We dared him to go and touch you! We thought you were an angel, because you had powder all over your face."

I said, "There was nothing on my face, I've worn makeup only once in my life."

That episode bothered me the whole week. That Saturday, we had a prayer meeting and there were thirty-five of us at the meeting. After we washed each other's feet, did communion, and worshipped, everybody had a white substance on their faces that looked like powder.

One night after entering God's Presence, I had an experience were I was in the sky riding what appeared to be a huge tricycle. I was aware that someone was there driving

These groanings cannot be heard, but can be translated and understood, but only by Him, if He will, and for His purpose!

Every time Jesus manifested to me, we would be talking but our mouths were not moving. I was always mindful that someone was there translating the conversation. That someone is the HOLY GHOST! He's amazing!

The INTELLIGENCE of the intelligent, HE IS POWER, and the source of it! So patient, loving and kind, His mannerism is PHENOMENAL! I love Him so much, and can talk about Him all day!

I'M ADDICTED TO HIM! He's the only person that intimidates me, and He's the most important person in the WORLD! He pours the love of God into our heart, counsels us, teaches us, protects us, and maintains our relationship with God! He even, transform our appearance, and allows us to see the transformed appearance of others.

A friend who was coming to town asked me to come to an engagement. After being in the Presence of Jesus all that day, I didn't want to go. After sitting there, debating, the Holy Spirit said, **"Go!"**

When I arrived, the person who invited me kind of gave me the cold shoulder. Sitting there alone, with hundreds of people around me, a stranger walked up and snapped my picture.

Then, someone came and waved in front of my face and walked off, but kept looking back at me. After a while, I decided to leave. The Holy Spirit stopped me and said, **"Go serve!"**

Although a physical kingdom will be set up on earth, in Jerusalem, during the thousand-year reign of Jesus; The spiritual Kingdom of God is in you and I.

> [20]Once, asked by the Pharisees when the kingdom of God would come, Jesus replied, The kingdom of God does not come with your careful observation, [21]nor will people say, 'Here it is,' or 'There it is,' because the kingdom of God is within you.
>
> Luke 17:20, 21

The kingdom of God is in the Holy Ghost, and the Holy Ghost is the kingdom of God! We can't even cast out demons without the Holy Ghost.

> If I cast out demons by the Spirit of God the kingdom of God has come upon you.
>
> Matthew 12:28

In deliverance we manifest the kingdom of God to the one being delivered, and the delivered receive the benefits of what the kingdom of God offers. The Holy Spirit is the author of the word of God. We can't understand the scripture without Him. He gives life to the letter we read.

> [20]No scripture is of no private interpretation, [21]for prophecy never had its origin in the will of man but holy men spoke boldly as they were carried along by the Holy Ghost.
>
> 2 Peter 1:20, 21

He intercedes in us! Our personal intercessor! He speaks a language that's without words in us, called groanings!

shall be established. Speak to a mountain, and it be removed. Cast out anything from anybody, because the power of God is resting on you from being in His Presence. If you don't get in His Presence, you have to wait to be quickened, to speak a promise, and it will manifest. If you're walking in the Spirit, you are allowed to do it at anytime.

Once I asked the Holy Spirit, "What does it mean to be in the Spirit?"

He responded, *"It is when you allow your spirit to be led by My Spirit, as I carry you along."*

On one occasion He said, *"When you are led by others, even yourself, you look for signs. But when you allow me to lead, signs follow you!"*

We can't do anything of spiritual value without God's Holy Spirit!

We are commanded in Romans 8:14, to be led by the Holy Ghost. Pray in the Spirit in Ephesians 6:18, walk in the Spirit in Galatians 5:16, worship in spirit and truth John 4:24, sing in our spirit 1 Corinthians 14:15, and be quickened by the Holy Ghost 1 Peter 3:18.

> We prophecy under His influence.
>
> Acts 2:17

> They spoke in tongues, as He enabled them.
>
> Acts 2: 4

> Our righteousness, joy, and peace is in the Holy Ghost! The kingdom of God is not a matter of meat and drink, but righteousness, peace, and joy in the Holy Ghost.
>
> Romans 14:17

THE OUTER COURT (BODY)

1. **GATE** ~ Jesus is our way in! Focus only on Him! All of your attention will be on Him, and your conversations with Him will be about Him, not your problems or situations. Only acknowledge Him during this moment.

2. **ALTAR OF SACRIFICE/BRONZE ALTAR~** Acknowledge what Jesus did for you by shedding His blood.

3. **BRONZE LAVER** ~ Pray the promises of God! Decree them over your life and the lives of others.

THE INNER COURT/HOLY PLACE
1st VEIL (SOUL)

4. **LAMPSTAND** ~ Surrender to Him your will, for His good, and perfect, and pleasing will.

5. **TABLE OF SHOWBREAD** ~ Surrender to the Holy Ghost. Surrender your all, ask Him to worship through you, and refill you.

6. **ALTAR OF INCENSE** ~ Worship!

THE INNER COURT HOLY OF HOLIES/MOST HOLY PLACE
2nd VEIL (SPIRIT)

7. **THE ARK OF THE COVENANT** ~ You are in the Presence of Jesus! BE SILENT! THE HOLY SPIRIT WILL SPEAK!!!

As you finish getting in His Presence and come out, you are now walking in the Spirit. You can decree a thing, and it

We serve a Triune God, and we ourselves are tri-part beings. We have a body that houses our soul and spirit. Our body represents the outer court, the soul the inner court, and our spirit the holy of holies. Our spirit is the holiest part of us, and is the only part of us that communicates with God!

Our spirit is the only part of us capable of conversing with God! He created us as spirit beings for the sake of communicating with Him.

Your spirit you knows you better than your soul you.

> Who among men know the thoughts of man except the man's spirit within him? In the same way no one knows the thoughts of God except God's Spirit.
>
> 1 Corinthians 2:11

One of the reasons blaspheming against the Holy Ghost is unforgivable is because The Holy Ghost — God's Breath, God's Spirit — is the Holiest part of Him. Our spirit is the holiest part of us, and this is why when a person is not born again or receives a born again spirit; it's unforgivable.

God is a Spirit! Jesus the Son represents His Body, God the Father Himself represents His Soul, and the Holy Ghost represents His Spirit!

The Holy Spirit is the one that leads us into God's Holy Presence. He's the one that helps us.

I'm under a ministry called The Administration of The Holy Spirit. In this ministry the Holy Spirit has instructed us to do demonstrations on how to enter the Presence of God. Below is a shortened version of how to enter His Presence.

both gifts and sacrifices, that could not make him that did the service perfect, as pertaining to the conscience.

Hebrews 9: 1-9

Moses was given instructions on how to build the tabernacle in the book of Exodus. God was very specific with His instructions. The Holy Ghost gave Moses the pattern for how we are to approach God. This pattern was a shadow, or type of what was to come. It was the old order/covenant, until the new order/covenant would come. The new order/covenant is found in Jesus.

The Jesus/Yeshua covenant is our new and better covenant. We no longer have to kill or shed the blood of an animal, sacrificing for our sin. Jesus is our Sacrificial Lamb. We no longer need a priest to serve as mediator between God and man. Jesus is our Mediator and High Priest who has made us a royal priesthood and a peculiar people.

In order for us to understand the new order, one must understand the old order. The old order is filled with shadows and types, but is an example, and served as a pattern for what we should do and expect now. The new is the most excellent and expedient way, although the old way was beneficial.

God gave Moses the pattern to teach the people how to approach Him. They had a physical tabernacle; we are the tabernacle. The physical tabernacle had three entranceways to get to the very Presence of God. These were: Outer Court, Inner Court, and Holy of Holies. With the Holy of Holies being the most holy part, the place where God would dwell and speak. It was a place where God would reveal Himself!

On the side of each elevator were stairs. I could see someone traveling on the stairs. Then, I was told to get on the elevator. When I made it to the second floor, I suddenly had on a uniform and was carrying a notebook in my hand. Then, I woke up.

Years later, the Holy Spirit gave me the interpretation of this dream, saying He was showing me the pattern into the Presence of Jesus. God is a God of patterns, types, symbols, numbers, shadows, principles, and parables. He's a mysterious God. I often tell Him how smart He is.

> [1]Then verily the first covenant had also ordinances of divine service, and a worldly sanctuary. [2]For there was a tabernacle made; the first, in which was the candlestick, and the table, and the showbread; which is called the sanctuary. [3]And after the second vail, the tabernacle which is called the Holiest of all; [4]Which had the golden censer, and the ark of the covenant overlaid around with gold, in which was the golden pot that had manna, and Aaron's rod that budded, and the tables of the covenant; [5]And over it the cherubim of glory shadowing the mercy-seat; of which we cannot now speak particularly.
>
> [6]Now when these things were thus ordained, the priests went always into the first tabernacle, accomplishing the service of God: [7]But into the second went the high priest alone once every year, not without blood, which he offered for himself, and for the errors of the people: [8]The Holy Spirit this signifying, that the way into the holiest of all was not yet made manifest, while the first tabernacle was yet standing: [9]Which was a figure for the time then present, in which were offered

are your god. Don't ever seek me for people. Seek Me only for Me!"

I had a dream I was standing outside this gate in front of a small building, waiting to go in. I opened the gate and stood on the grounds looking around. It looked like a campus because of the university-type buildings. I was trying to get to the further away, bigger building for some reason.

Then, the Holy Spirit spoke, ***"You must go through here first, before you get there."***

As I went into the building, The Holy Spirit said, ***"You must wash here."***

After washing in a silver basin, I remember looking at some furniture in the small building with limited space. The place had no windows, and it was dim inside. As I looked ahead, I saw a wall, and muttered, "How can I get around that wall? I don't see a door."

The Holy Spirit said, ***"I will help you."***

Then, I felt my body being pulled to the floor. After lying on the floor, looking up at the ceiling for a while, a crack appeared across the bottom of the wall, with light illuminating from that other room.

The light was shining on the floor where I was laying, making the crack obvious. I rolled through the crack, into the room. The next thing I knew, I was in the university. It looked like three universities stacked on top of each other. I saw transparent elevators that looked thirty feet high, each transporting one to the other, with floors attached to each at the thirty-foot level.

CHAPTER NINETEEN

Intimacy Beyond Ecstasy

Getting in the Presence of Jesus is everything, and everything is in His Presence. Our protection, illuminations, joy, peace, love, fulfillment, favor, provisions, prosperity, revelations, inspirations, and much more are in His Presence! He reveals Himself when we get in His Presence.

For me, it's an addiction! When I'm there, nothing and no one is more important to me. I learned how to discipline myself, and to get in His Presence daily from my sister Amanda. The Holy Spirit put the desire in me to do so, but I had to learn the proper way by studying. When we get in God's Presence, we do so to seek Him, not things and not for people.

Once I got in His Presence, with intentions of seeking Him for three pastors who needed answers ASAP!

The Holy Spirit said, *"Don't seek me for people! You speak over your own life, intercede for others, but never seek Me for people! When you seek Me for people, they*

I jumped up and went and got more study material to learn exactly what worship was! Oh my!!! What an experience worship brings. Every time there was a problem, I would get in worship! When He revealed something in His word, I would worship! After prayer, I would worship! God's peace was released to me as I worshipped! Worship kept my focus on Jesus and not my problems.

During that time, my husband and I went a year and six months without paying our mortgage! They sent me letters of foreclosure, and I would worship! We still have our home, and made history with the unbelievable, unheard of interest rate we have. Glorrrrrry!!! We struggled for five years!

Now, I'm grateful for that struggle, because it allowed me to develop a closer relationship with Jesus, delivered me from pride, and showed me how to experience God's presence daily through WORSHIP!!!

In our Bible Study one Wednesday night, the study guide was on entering the presence of God. After I got home, I bowed and began loving on God. Then, the big face appeared.

After sitting there looking at it for a while, as it looked at me, I whispered, "Lord what is this big face?"

He said, *"It is My face."*

I asked, "Where is your body?"

He responded, *"You are My body. You see My face because you are in My Presence."*

After getting home one night, found out my washer, refrigerator, and heating unit were all broken. We'd been having problems with them for a while, but had no money to get them repaired. We had a bag of rice, an onion, and a loaf of bread; and I had just spent the last money we had to fill up our cars for the week, and buy three packs of chicken to last us through the week. It was so cold outside that it made the inside of our home cold. I told my boys to wash up, and sleep in their coats, then I bundled them up in quilts.

After everyone left the next morning, I sat on the couch in tears, asking God, "Did I do something wrong? Will I ever get a breakthrough?"

All of a sudden, I felt the Presence of the Holy Spirit, in mid air, behind my couch in the walkway. As a vision of Him appeared in front of me, that showed Him lingering behind me, He whispered, *"Write what you see!"*

After I finished, the vision disappeared.

Then He spoke, *"As you worship, I will resolve every situation that has your focus."*

Things got even worse, but I didn't want to ask my mom for help. I was dealing with pride, and had always been very self-sufficient. I kept saying, "I'm not sharing my business with anyone." Besides, I believed you shouldn't ask anyone for help, but should help yourself.

Looking in from the outside, no one would have never known we were struggling. I still went to Church every week, studied, prayed, and worked for God. My pastor asked me often if everything was okay, and each time I would get mad, but say. "Yes, sir."

One day, my pastor called, saying very politely, "Sister Spurlock, the Lord let me know you are dealing with pride. Ask Him to help you."

After hanging up with him, I said, "I am not dealing with pride!"

Immediately the Holy Spirit said, **"Yes you are, and you're dealing with it right now!"**

So, I started to cry, saying, "How? Please deliver me!" What I called being independent and self sufficient, The Holy Spirit called pride! Then, I became ashamed, saying, "You want me to share my hardships with others, but they will know my business."

He let me know that if my business was not *His* business, then don't share it. "But if I allow my business to become His business, then my business will become His priority."

The desire in me to know Him was getting stronger. I started prostrating myself for hours in silence after studying and prayer, just to be in His presence. I began asking Him daily to let me be in His presence.

For two months, when I went to church I would see this big face. Then, I started seeing it in my room.

On the second day of February, I lost my job. I was on salary at that job and had made exactly what He asked me to give up each week! I was devastated! Plus, we were in the middle of purchasing another home. A week prior to closing, the bank called and said I needed $18, 000!

I cried and cried, saying, "I can't come up with that kind of money!" I had lost one of my jobs, so I couldn't go get a loan, and had no one to borrow that kind of money from. I called my pastor and shared my situation, and he gave me a person's name, saying God just told him to give it to me.

After I hung up, I vowed, "I will not ask a person I don't know for that kind of money." Two days went by, and the lender kept calling. I kept delaying the process.

Finally, I picked up the phone book, looking for the person's name, found out the person was a business owner. Went to the business, but the secretary said I needed an appointment.

Just then, someone came from the back office. I asked them if they were the person I was looking for. They said yes, and I told them what I needed. Then, I promised to pay them back with interest. They looked at the secretary, and told her to cut a check for me. Then they looked at me and said, "God bless you. Have a wonderful day!"

After a year had passed, we had to file bankruptcy. My husband was bringing home literally $1 a week from one of his jobs, and the weekend job he had along with the job I had, barely gave us enough money for utilities, gas, and food for the children after paying the mortgage.

Then, my income was cut in half because the Holy Spirit told me not to charge people for the work He required me to do for them. He only wanted me to render the services, lay hands and pray for the people, then let them leave without paying.

CHAPTER EIGHTEEN

In His Presence

One of the greatest things I've learned is how to enter God's presence His way. Years before I learned this, I spent most of my time learning to hear His voice, knowing Him, learning who He created me to be, and the things I needed to be delivered from. Even now, daily I seek Him to have a deeper relationship with Him.

Shortly after giving my life to Him, I found myself not wanting to work two jobs anymore so I could have more time alone with Him. On New Year's Eve, I made a vow to God saying I would do whatever He wanted me to do to fellowship with Him more.

On New Year's Day, the Holy Spirit said, **"Give your pastor a thousand dollars,"** but I totally ignored this. I thought to myself, *Oh no, I can't give up that much money, I work hard for it. Besides, he doesn't need my money; I pay tithes. Don't they pay him?*

The Holy Ghost spoke everyday for the next thirty days, saying, **"Give him a thousand dollars."** I just couldn't do it.

I approached the next stoplight, to get on the highway. The Holy Spirit said, **"Don't be foolish, put your hands on the wheel."**

My grandmother lived about fifteen minutes from where I lived. After arriving at my grandma's, I saw she had three relatives from out of town there visiting her. All three accepted Jesus into their hearts.

Joy flooded me, and I began to laugh uncontrollably. The doctor came in and said all my tests looked good. I was so full of joy that I just nodded my head with a "yes".

I saw the doctor watching me as I walked out. As I got in my truck, it was as if I had been drinking alcohol. When I got home, I stumbled into my house and lay down on my bed, laughing and saying, "Why do I feel like I'm intoxicated?"

Shortly thereafter, I started yawning and becoming very sleepy. Suddenly, an Angel appeared as if wind was upon it. As the wind from the Angel filled my room, my curtains began to sway, papers fell to the floor, and my clothes on my body began to move. Then, the Holy Spirit said, **"Go to your grandmother's house. They are waiting for you."**

I told Him, "I can't drive. I'm sleepy."

But He said, **"I sent you help."**

I stumbled to my truck, cranked it, and put it in reverse. Then I leaned my head back, and put my feet on the brake. Even though the brake was on, my truck began moving backwards up the small hill, exiting out into the street.

I raised my head; it was if someone was sitting in my lap! The gear moved to drive, and my truck started moving again. I was laughing so hard, and was shocked by what was happening!

I went through the third stop sign with my hands lifted to heaven, shouting, "Someone is driving my truck!" I passed a lady and her sister, and I stuck both my hands out the window, yelling, "I'm not driving!"

I went through a fourth stop sign, then two red lights. When I got in front of the doctor's office, (the doctor I had just left) I said, "Look! Look! I'm not driving." Then I said, "Wow! This is crazy!"

I kept screaming, telling every person I passed that I wasn't driving. My hands were hanging out the window as

When we finished, it was after 5 a.m. that morning, the day of my appointment. I was to be there at 8 a.m., so I went home, ate breakfast and got dressed before going to the doctor's office.

As I sat there waiting for them to call my name, I became nervous. They called me into the room and ran different tests. Then asked me to wait in the room until the results came in. As I lay there wondering if something was wrong and what would the doctor say, The Lord spoke, **"Lay back on the table."**

I said to Him, "Lord, I trust You, and no matter what happens here today, I still love You."

As I lay back in total silence, I felt His presence hovering over my head. I didn't see any angels but I saw a mist over my head. It was not as thick as it had been at my mom's. Then I heard a voice saying, **"There is nothing wrong with you. Be calm, I'm with you!"**

I was unsure who was speaking to me. I had just learned the Lord's voice maybe a year or so ago, but still wrestled with whether what I was hearing was Him speaking. I was in doubt because it was exactly what I wanted to hear. My pastor taught us that when we're unsure of who's speaking, ask, "Did Jesus come in the flesh?"

At any rate, when I heard that, I said, "Who are you?"
He answered, **"The Holy Spirit."**
I replied, "For real?"
He said, **"Yes, It is I."**
So I asked, "Did Jesus come in the flesh?"
He replied, **"Yes."**
Amazed, I then said, "You are talking to me?"
He said, **"It Is I who speaks to you!"**

CHAPTER SEVENTEEN

It is I

I was concerned with changes that were taking place in my body, and decided to set a doctor's appointment. The day prior to the appointment, I called my mom and shared my concerns with her. I told her I hadn't slept in two days, and she invited me to come spend the night with her so she could pray over me and I could rest.

Around 7 p.m., I arrived at my mom's. When I entered her home, there was an atmosphere of peace that made me want to rest. My mother prayed, asking God to touch my body as I lay there on her couch in silence. She then asked me to get my bible so we could look up scriptures on the promises pertaining to healing.

After reading, we began to praise and worship God. Mother then played soft music. As I listened, I dosed off for maybe thirty minutes. When I awakened, the house seemed to be filled with a mist. I looked over at my mom and she was still bowed in worship, so I got on the floor beside her, lifted my hands and joined in.

I saw another nurse who had also come in to take the lady's vitals, so I asked her. She said no one but her checked the patient's vitals. I described the nurse to her, and she said she might work on another floor. I asked if she could check that for us. She did, and no one by that name worked at that hospital.

God has angels and so does satan.

> And there was war in heaven. Michael and his angels fought against the dragon, and the dragon and his angels fought back.
>
> Revelation 12:7

from departing this life. We stood in her room for hours, and nurses came in and out checking her. While we were standing at the side of her bed, suddenly angels swarmed the room. As my sister and I watched them, they seemed as if they were positioning themselves.

Another nurse walked in, she was fairly nice, but her presence was giving me an uneasy feeling. She had come in about three times, and the last time she checked the woman's vitals she asked if she could get us something to drink. After she left, I told Amanda I didn't get a good feeling about that nurse and I didn't know why.

Amanda suggested we sing praises to God. We did, and after we praised, we just started worshipping and then got silent. The nurse came back, but this time it seemed like she was supernaturally restricted from coming in the room. She stood at the door, and I read her name badge as she walked out backwards. After that, we decided to leave and visit the lady's relatives.

On our way back to the hospital with one of the lady's relatives in the truck with us, another angel appeared. The relative screamed when they saw the angel following the truck. Suddenly, the angel stopped, but we kept going. After arriving at the hospital, the lady soon went to be with the Lord.

As I stood outside her room, thanking God for the help and support of the medical staff, I said, "I thank you for quickening the nurse to get us something to drink."

God spoke, saying, **"She's not mine. I didn't send her."**

I told my sister what the Lord said, then went to the nursing station to ask for the nurse. They said no one by that name worked on this floor. So, I went to the break room and asked the other nurses about her. They said the same. Baffled, I walked back to the room.

> See that you do not look down on one of these little ones. For I tell you that their angels in heaven always see the face of my father in heaven.
>
> Matthew 18:10

Angel assigned to every family.

> Genesis chapters 18 and 19

Angel assigned to every state and nation.

> Daniel 12:1

Assigned to every city and Church.

> Revelations chapters 2 and 3

We are not to worship them, nor can we get rid of them. Sometimes they are not gender recognizable, some look human, some do not, they even take on the appearance of others.

> And all that sat in the council, looking steadfastly on him (Stephen), saw his face as it had been the face of an angel.
>
> Acts 6:15

They often go unnoticed, but are everywhere at all times, and will manifest. They are at hospitals, funeral services, and medical clinics. When I go pray for the hospitalized sick, or if a person's life here on earth is almost over, there are always two that will appear. I don't know why there are two, but two manifest. They assist in a person's departure from this life. I've seen them take a person into heaven.

I've also seen those who are not God's angels. Once, Amanda and I went to pray for a lady who was hours away

table, but didn't know what to do. Their presence had become overwhelming. Because I lacked understanding, I became frustrated.

Once, while sitting at my desk at work, four appeared. I came out of my office, and went to sit in the waiting area. I was very annoyed, so I grabbed the bible in an attempt to read something, hoping maybe I would get a rhema word from God to utter, but didn't.

Two of the angels stood in front of me, and I started yelling, "What do you want me to do? What do you want from me? God, please make this stop! I don't know what to do! What is your purpose for showing up? I don't know what to say!"

Frustrated, I opened the bible and it landed on Exodus 23. My eyes went directly to the 20th verse, so I started reading verses 20-22. After reading that, I knew it was time for me to study about angels.

After reading those scriptures, what stood out was my Name is in Him. The Him this scripture was referring to was Jesus. The Angel on the bus trip with me was Jesus himself, or what some call a theophany, meaning a self-manifestation.

Jesus was also referred to in the bible as The Angel of the Lord. In 1 Corinthians 10:1-4 Paul stated that Jesus accompanied them when the children of Israel passed through the Red Sea. Exodus 13: 21 lets us know the Lord went ahead of them. In Exodus 3:2, Jesus is called the Angel of the Lord. In Genesis 32 Jacob wrestled with The Angel of the Lord who was the Lord Himself.

In studying about the angels, I learned that they will appear, protect us, guide us, talk, participate in deliverance, guard us, go ahead of us, do God's bidding, worship God, listen, and respond to the word of God spoken through us. There is an angel assigned to every person including children.

> So is my word that goes forth out from my mouth:
> It will not return to me empty, but will accomplish what I desire and achieve the purpose for which I sent it.
>
> Isaiah 55:11

God's word in our mouth that will achieve the purpose for which it is sent out, is his rhema word.

I used to quote scripture after scripture. I was not in the Spirit; I was just quoting scriptures. I learned the scriptures, but the promises of those scriptures were not manifesting. This discouraged me! If He said it, I believed it. But what was I doing wrong that was causing me not to see what He said?

Then the Holy Spirit spoke saying, **"It's when My word goeth forth out of My mouth. My mouth has to be speaking out of your mouth, before you see My word performed."**

God's word can be presented in two forms: logo and rhema. His logo word is His said word, while His rhema is His saying word. His rhema is His word that keeps coming to you, or that He keeps bringing to your remembrance. This can also be a rhema song. A song you're reminded of throughout your day. When you receive the rhema, the promise that's attached to it is available for you at that moment.

Finally, after a partial understanding of the angels' purpose, I became hungry for a rhema word from God daily so that when they appeared, I could speak the word. Then, when I received a rhema, the angels didn't manifest, and when they manifested, I didn't receive a rhema word. This discouraged me, so in a sense I was right back where I started.

They would appear and I would remain silent. I would see them in service, but didn't know what to do. On numerous occasions, I saw the smaller ones around the offering

I then said, "What about me?"

Then a voice behind me said, "I'm here for you."

I looked and saw one standing behind me. I said, "So, y'all can talk?" For seven years when I'd seen them, they had never uttered a word. I knew they spoke back in bible days, and knew that one talked with me on the bus, but some kind of way I blocked out that they would speak now. The one on the bus was the one I touched, and looked like a physical human until the end, but the ones that I was seeing now were aglow and looked supernatural.

Instantly when I said, "So ya'll can talk?" they began speaking in a different language. The only word I made out was the word lama.

After making it home, I looked up the word lama. One interpretation mean forsaken. So, I believed the angel was letting me know I was not forsaken.

> If I speak in the tongues of men and of angels, but have not love, I am only a resounding gong or a clanging cymbal.
>
> 1 Corinthians 13:1

In prayer that night, I said to the Lord, "The angels talked. Why didn't you tell me they talk? Is it safe to say something to them? Why do they look so serious?"

He instructed me to read these passages:

> Praise the Lord, you his angels, you mighty ones who do his bidding, who obey his word. Angels hearken to the voice of God's word.
>
> Psalm 103: 20 (NIV)

At first, they startled me. I questioned myself, trying to figure out if what I was seeing was real and wondering what they were. I remember asking God, "Am I having some kind of melt down? Do I need to seek professional help?"

The more I asked Him to not let me see them, the more they manifested. I would literally see them moving alongside the people in churches, grocery stores, shopping centers, on my job, and in my home. Sometimes people would walk up and start talking to me and they would appear.

Once, I went to look at a home and about twelve traveled alongside the truck. As the truck moved, they moved! On many occasions, I would see them with containers in their hands. I've seen them with what look like whistles up to their mouths, too. They don't seem to care that I see them, because they never stop doing what they were sent to do. They would look right at me, but kept working.

This happened for about seven years before I learned their purpose. By this time, I'd just started accepting it as apart of the norm.

During those times, I would say to the Lord, "Why are You allowing me to see this?" Up to that point I'd only heard them speak twice. One of those times was during the bus trip. The other time, my sister and I were walking together. She started walking ahead of me, and an angel moved swiftly behind her.

As I moved to catch up with them, I decided to say something to the angel. I'd never heard them speak within the seven years, and didn't know if I should say something to them because they always had an intense look on their faces. This time I spoke.

I said, "What are you doing here?"

The Angel said, "I'm here for her," pointing to my sister.

CHAPTER SIXTEEN

Angels Galore

For he has given his angels charge over thee, to keep thee in all thy ways.

Psalm 91:11

Bless the Lord, ye his angels that excel in strength, that do his commandments, hearkening unto the voice of his word.

Psalm 103:20 (KJV)

Are not all angels ministering spirits sent to serve those who will inherit salvation?

Hebrews 1:14

The first Angel encounter I had and was fully aware of was on my bus trip to Chicago in November 1992. The second time was while sitting in Church. My pastor stated they were there recording during tithes and offerings, and two manifested. After that experience at Church, I began seeing them consistently.

As we stood up, watching it move farther away from us, it flipped over and became a huge cloud.

I was sitting at my bar reading Exodus 24:10 where it states, "And they saw the God of Israel: and there was under his feet as it were a paved work of a sapphire stone, and as it were the body of heaven in his clearness."

Sitting there, I said very softly, "God if they saw You, what did you look like?" Instantly, a vision of a huge Cloud appeared! I flipped backwards off my bar stool, landing on the floor. Then, I was under the power of God in my tongue language for what seemed like hours.

At service one Sunday, a lady in a wheelchair was there. The power of God fell upon me and I fell to the floor. As I lay there, He told me to lay my hands on the lady's feet. I uttered, "No, Lord, I don't want to be out of order in this ministry."

He said, *"I have a ministry, too!"*

After I touched her, the lady got up and started walking.

I arrived home, puzzled. I wondered, *Why did He ask me to break order?*

Then He said, *"Would you like to be a part of My ministry?"* He then instructed us to study on the Cloud and Fire that led the Children of Israel in the wilderness.

In April 2016, He instructed us to do a forty-day fast in preparation for the Glory that will invade the earth. He called it a Glory Collision! As we would meet house to house, The Holy Spirit would perform the miraculous! As we studied, The Holy Spirit revealed so many things to us pertaining to His Shekinah Glory!

During that time, I had a dream we were standing on a beach like we were picking up some shells. Directly across the street, in front of the beach, were mountains. I heard a noise, and looked towards the mountain. There, I saw a huge round image on fire, but it had eyes forming. It formed completely, and after it finished it started moving swiftly toward us!

I yelled, "Everybody lay down!" but they acted like they didn't hear me. I then started running towards them, in an attempt to tell them to lie down. By that time, the great ball of fire was upon on me and picked me up off my feet. As violent as it appeared, it laid me down very gently.

As the others lay down, it hovered over their heads, then started moving in the opposite direction from which it came.

CHAPTER FIFTEEN

He Jumped In

In the fall of 2003, I saw a cloud about the size of a cantaloupe with eyes and a mouth about ten feet from me. Suddenly, the cloud leapt at me. As it did this, I grabbed my husband around the neck. Then, the cloud leaped on me! It happened so fast that I didn't have time to think.

When He leaped on me, my husband and I rolled out of the bed onto the floor, and then under the bed. Then we rolled into the bathroom, then back to the bedroom and back under the bed. We rolled and rolled and rolled, tumbling over each other.

When we finally came to a stop, we lay there for a minute before we said anything. He responded first, "What in the world just happened?"

I said, "I don't know." After that, I burst out crying. Later, I found out that the cloud was the Holy Spirit.

In 2014, the Lord changed our prayer ministry's name to "The Administration of the Holy Spirit." This came about as a result of what happened in a Church service.

doing that, and sometimes I would hear yes and sometimes I would hear, no, no, no!

This is how you can recognize the Spirit of God:

> [2]...every spirit that acknowledges that Jesus Christ has come in the flesh is from God, [3]but every spirit that does not acknowledge Jesus is not from God.
>
> 1 John 4:2, 3

Someone standing with Him or in Him was doing the talking. Who the Person was, I couldn't see.

He said, *"You want to see My Glory? Open your hands, you are My Glory!"*

After opening my hands, light was in my hands.

Then He said, *"My Glory is upon you! Whatever you bind on earth is bound in heaven, whatever you loose on earth is loosed in heaven!"*

Then He faded away.

Afterwards, during my prayer time I began asking Him to teach me how to hear his voice more clearly and to understand what He was speaking so I could share with others that they may hear Him, too.

Months went by, and I was headed to service. The Holy Spirit said, *"When you are asked how to know when I'm speaking, tell them it's according to how much one reads what I said."*

In service, the pastor said the scripture about binding and loosing. As I wrote it down, I started whispering, "This is really a scripture. Jesus said this to me, but I didn't realize it was a scripture. I hadn't yet read it, or heard it before."

After service, I went up to the pastor and asked him what the scripture meant. He explained, then asked me what was I reading. I told him the book of Daniel. He said, "I'm glad you ask questions, but you need to invest in a Study Bible." He then asked, "What kind of bible do you have?" I told him it was a devotional Bible my sister had given me."

The next day, I purchased a Study Bible. As I continued to study, I realized Jesus might have said a lot of things to me, but I didn't know it was Him speaking because I didn't know His word.

My pastor also said if I was unsure of who was talking to me, then I should ask if Jesus came in the flesh. I began

CHAPTER FOURTEEN

Show Me Your Glory

After that, my prayer life changed. I stopped asking for stuff, and started asking for Him. I spent a lot of time reading, and then listening. I would often ask Him to show me His Glory.

I had received a letter in the mail from a church that read, *"Jesus is passing through."* So, I began saying in prayer, "As you pass through, show me Your Glory."

This particular night, I lay at the foot of the bed and closed my eyes, turning on my side to go to sleep. I repeated over and over, "Show me Your Glory."

Jesus revealed Himself again, and was standing there radiant. His eyes were so piercing, and made me feel like I was transparent before Him. It was if He knew my thoughts at that very moment. His clothing was bright, but not as nearly as bright as His countenance.

The energy that radiated from His Being made the hairs on my body stand! As I sat there in awe of His glowing Presence, the light from His glory illuminated my room. He started speaking, but again, His mouth was not moving.

My paw paw died in January 2007, two years before Amina was born. I went over salvation vows with him, and saw him being transported to heaven when he died. I'll never forget the look on his face as he was entering heaven! It was priceless!

My paw paw was a good father, husband grandfather, and hard worker. When he died, he left 75 grandchildren, great grandchildren, and great-great grands behind who loved him and missed him very much. He really took care of all of us; loving us equally.

what happened, she told them that when the wreck happened, Elder Rawls stopped her and another little girl from going out the window. She said he stood in front of the window, caught them, and sat them on the floor.

I said, "Amina, Elder Rawls was not on the bus."

She said, "Yes, ma'am, he was, and he had on a white cape." Amina said the same thing to everyone who took her statement.

After we got home, my husband and I talked with her and she still said Elder Rawls caught her.

After I shared this with Scherry, she reminded me about my bus trip. Elder Rawls is our pastor, the same person the Angel on the bus resembled.

Shenitha came to live with us for a while. One day, Amina told her there was someone standing in the room, near the bed. As I went to the room, she said a big bright light was standing in the room, and she pointed to the light. I didn't see it, but believed she did.

Amina, often times, would go off by herself to a quiet place to read. Once, while she was sitting and reading, she said," "Mama, Paw Paw Pat is grandma Shelia's daddy."

I said, "Yes, Amina. Who told you about Paw Paw Pat?

She said, "He told me he was grandma Shelia's daddy, and he told me to tell you hello."

I stopped curling my hair, and sat down thinking about how to respond, and whether she really saw my paw paw.

She said, "Mama, he said to tell you to let my daddy wear that white suit you have that was his."

CHAPTER THIRTEEN

Amina

December 25, 2009, I went into labor at 28 weeks. They stopped the labor pains, but she was born two days later. Amina was born premature, so she spent the next nine weeks in the in University Hospital. Five times she stopped breathing, and each time I would sing, *"El Shaddai, El Shaddai, El Elyon my Adonai, age to age You're still the same, by the power of Your Name."*

That very last time she stopped breathing, they gave up on her, but I didn't. I knew God would bring her out! I reminded myself of a dream God showed me, walking in our backyard holding her hand, and being pregnant with my youngest son.

And besides during prayer one night, the Lord told me she would be filled with wisdom from birth, so when she was born, I held on to that promise. I would go in her room every day, pray with her, sing, and read to her. God brought her through it.

At the age of four, she was in a van accident with the school she attended. When they took her statement about

hearing Him speak to me more and more about me. I sought Him daily about helping me to overcome me. I wanted Him to remove anything in my life that would prevent me from developing a closer relationship with Him.

One night I was praying, asking God what was His plan for my life and what He would have me do. I sat there in quietness for maybe an hour after praying, then Jesus appeared! When He manifested, I hid under a blanket.

"Don't be afraid," I said to myself as I slowly slid the blanket from my face. There He stood! When I looked at Him, I felt like He was looking at me and seeing my past, present and future all in my right now.

I felt as though He saw me when I was a child and chewed that bubble gum I'd gotten out of the pack in the grocery store. The shame I was feeling at that moment caused me to feel embarrassed.

He was talking to me, but His mouth was not moving! Although I didn't see anyone else, I was aware that someone else was present with Him, translating to me what He was saying. He said, *"Ask me for what you want."* He then waited for me to respond.

When I didn't say anything, He asked, *"What is it you want me to do for you?"*

Out of all the things I thought I wanted or had been asking for, I couldn't think of a thing, nor did I want anything at that time. As I sat there looking steadily and intently at the brilliance of His Being, I said, "I just want You."

He smiled, then disappeared.

I had a client to tell me, I was not going to heaven because I wore my scrub suits to work. As she came monthly for her appointment, she would say this to me. I started to tune her out, but she was making the other clients feel bad. The clients He allowed me to witness to about how much He loves them and desired for them to accept Him. I prayed to the Lord concerning this, but got no answer.

One day, as she came in for her appointment, she approached the glass entry doors, about fifteen feet from me. As she came up, the Holy Spirit said, **"Point your finger at her!"** I did, and she fell backwards on the pavement!

Everyone started screaming and running to get out the door to help her. I yelled, "Stop! Nobody move."

As I walked outside, He said, **"Cast out cancer."**

I stood over her, telling the cancer to let loose of her! After helping her up, she shared with me that she had just left her doctor's appointment and had been diagnosed with third stage cancer. Only she and her doctor knew this. She'd stopped by to cancel her appointment with me so she could go talk to her husband about the diagnosis.

This lady had disowned her daughter because she started wearing pants. This was the same feeling she had about my scrubs. The scriptures teach us to know the word of God and avoid foolishness. When she would say things like that, I ignored her, but it started bothering others, so it bothered me, too.

I often remind myself to share with the people what God wants them to have, and not what I think a person needs.

As the Lord delivered me from a religious spirit, I became more compassionate and loving towards others. I started

> All scripture is given by inspiration of God, and is profitable for doctrine, for reproof, for correction, for instruction in righteousness.
>
> 2 Timothy 3:16

We should use the scriptures for these particular things, but not neglect the other scriptures, including pray for them, encourage them, teach them, accept those whose faith is weak without passing judgment, helping to restore each other, being long suffering, patient with one another, and last but not least, love.

Before this, I had no balance, only correction. I didn't think about what God brought me out of, or the mercy He showed me when I was a capital good sinner. He taught me about extending to others the same mercy He showed me. I love God's people and understand that His plan is to save them and cleanse them.

My job is to catch them. We can't force God on people, or scare them into serving Him, because if we do and they accept Him because they're scared, after a while they will backslide. To remedy this, teach them to respect and love Him.

A person will not hurt someone they respect, and will not stay with someone they don't love. A person that stays with someone they don't love, ends up using them. I learned that I couldn't make my husband serve God. As the befitting cliché goes, "you can lead a horse to the water but you can't make him drink."

the Lord, asking, "How do you expect me to stay with him while his lifestyle is something I despise?"

I began telling Him everything I thought was wrong with my husband. After I got quiet, Jesus spoke, ***"How dare you judge another man's servant?"***

I responded saying, "He's not Your servant. He doesn't even serve you."

He replied, ***"A servant doesn't know his master's business but a friend does. That's why I call you friend, friend!"***

This was the day I got delivered from resentment towards my husband. The cliché, "one word from Jesus will change your situation," was really in affect that day. The Holy Spirit told me that I was not fully cleansed, that's why I pointed out sin in my husband. I was doing this not only to him, but others as well. I began focusing on how I could become cleansed, and doing this took my focus off of seeing how others needed to be cleansed.

At Bible Study that following week, my pastor gave out sheets titled, "How to Know if You Have a Religious Spirit." I understood how to identify if a person had a religious spirit, but wanted to know how one developed it, and what Jesus thought about it.

In my mind, I thought being religious was what Jesus/Yeshua wanted. After looking over the study guide, the first sentence that got my attention was pointing out the sins of others. I repented, and asked God for forgiveness.

I almost destroyed my marriage taking the scriptures and using them daily to point out my husband's sins. I asked my husband for forgiveness and vowed to not do that again.

marriage, that others often would say to me. After hearing it quoted, just like this: "God said, A saved wife will bring about a saved husband." I believed it to be so.

Even when I read 2 Corinthians 7:10 -14, all I could see while reading was what I heard from others.

That day, I shouted out to God in anger, saying, "You said my husband would be won over because of me being saved. You said a saved wife will bring about a saved husband."

The Holy Spirit responded, saying, "*I didn't say that, Paul said that*"

I was literally shocked! I didn't know if I was shocked because of what He said, or because I finally heard Him speak to me. Instantly I grabbed my bible, it flipped directly to 2 Corinthians the 7th chapter. Paul said twice, "I and not the Lord," between the 10th and 14th verses.

I ran into the den shouting, "Honey, the Lord spoke to me!" But my husband was so angry with me that he just walked out. I was so grateful that He spoke to me that I was no longer upset.

I started telling God, "You really talk! Thank You for letting me hear You."

Most of the conversations I had with my husband were telling him how God didn't like the things he was doing. Everyday, I pointed out a sin that was in his life according to the word. Because of this, we started growing farther and farther apart.

My husband was good to me, the destructive things he did had nothing to do with me — they were all what he was doing to himself. He was, and is even now, the perfect husband, father, and friend.

I began asking the Lord how to fix my marriage, but everything I did was not enough. One evening, I cried out to

CHAPTER TWELVE

Ask Me For What You Want

For weeks during my prayer time I had been asking for so many things, financially, spiritually, and physically. I longed for intimacy with Jesus, and to hear Him speak to me. I was not mature enough yet to discern when He was talking to me, but I felt His Presence daily, with some days being stronger than others.

Now that I was delivered from fear, I wanted to be alone so no one would distract me during my time with the Lord. Apparently, this offended my husband to a certain degree, because our relationship began to change. I became bitter towards him for not changing, and he began to despise me because I had changed.

One day after a disagreement my husband and I were discussing getting a divorce. I went in the bedroom, closed the door and started quoting to God a promise I heard about

On that third day my sister-in-law went into labor, and was rushed to the hospital. The umbilical cord was wrapped around the baby's neck, so she was immediately, rushed into surgery. As I was running behind them, putting on the suit required to enter the surgical room, the nurse shouted, "We can't get a heartbeat!"

As the baby came out, he wasn't breathing. After the doctor tried relentlessly to revive the baby, he shook his head and asked the nurse to call the time of death. As I held my sister-in-law's hand, looking up at the doctor, everything became silent! I couldn't hear again!

After a few minutes, as I watched their lips move, I could feel the power of God intensify upon on me. I walked over to where the baby was and placed my hand over his heart. I started speaking in a language that I had no idea I spoke, and I for sure didn't know what I was saying. All of a sudden, the baby started sneezing! After that, I could hear the medical staff and the machines.

The nurse shouted, "It's a miracle! It's a miracle!" The doctor, who was standing there with papers in his hand, rushed over and started checking the baby.

As for me, power was flowing so heavily in my body that I decided to step out so I could praise God aloud. As I approached the door, the nurse was about to swipe her badge to let me out, but the doctor turned and said, "No, let her stay!"

He then asked me to come over and place my hand over the plastic like material, while he worked on the baby. God did the supernatural, in one of the most unfavorable situations. This baby is now a teenager and very smart.

I went into my son's room, where my two boys, niece and nephew were asleep. I anointed them and was about to walk out the door, when the Holy Spirit said, ***"Look at your son."***

I pulled the blankets off him and it looked like someone was pulling his body up off the bed, and then dropping him back onto it. This happened repeatedly, so I sat on his back, anointing him with oil. I had forgotten they had a friend sleeping over that night.

I had no clue of what I was doing. The television came on with the volume full blast, as it had in my bedroom earlier, but this time the young lady who had walked into my room earlier was on my son's television, dancing and saying, "I got the spirit!"

I turned the television off, went into the next room, and saw my cousin was having a seizure. I anointed him, and he stopped seizing. After that, I prayed and read the rest of the night.

That night the spirit of fear was broken by God, allowing me to come face to face with the one who made me fearful — the devil. That night, the Holy Spirit gave me power to fight and overcome fear. Thank you, Yeshua! The thing that bound me for almost thirty years was broken!!!

Before that, the fear was so bad that my husband would have to get up in the middle of the night and get me something to drink if I was thirsty. When I got off work at night, he would have to wait to go to bed until I got home, so he could meet me on the porch. I would never stay at home alone at night. Thank God, I was set free that night! I felt like a live wire, and didn't eat or sleep for the next three days.

I was awake for those three days, and felt like electricity was flowing inside me as a result of the fire and cloud balls that entered into me.

I could hardly get words out, but finally asked, "Why didn't you answer me before? I needed you — something was in here! Can you get me something to drink?

As he got out of bed to walk to the kitchen, I shouted, "Stop! Turn the TV on." He did, but the family movie I inserted earlier was playing.

I jumped out of bed, following him into the kitchen. I told him to check the laundry room, and turn all of the lights on. Nothing was there.

After we got back in bed, I called Trina and Amanda, but neither of them answered. Next, I called my mom. She answered on the first ring, saying, "What's wrong?"

I proceeded to tell her, "Mother you're not going to believe what just happened to me—"

She interrupted me, and it didn't sound like her voice. "He's not gone yet. He's still in the house. Anoint your home."

I said okay and hung up the phone. "He's gone," I said aloud. "I got him out of here, and saw him leave. Besides, I left my anointing oil in my truck."

All of a sudden, balls of fire the size of oranges began dropping from my ceiling into my body. Then the fireballs changed to what looked like cotton balls about the same size. I didn't know what it was at the time, so I started dodging them. They followed me as I ran around the room, and as they entered into me, strength came into my body.

At that moment the Holy Spirit said, *"He's in there with your children. Go! Anoint your home."*

I thought He was telling me to get the oil and anoint my home, but later found out the anointing was upon me and all I had to do was walk through my home. I walked outside, got my oil out of the truck, came back in, and started anointing my home.

Suddenly, the television changed stations to a scary movie. I didn't own any scary movies, nor would I watch them when visiting others.

The volume on the television was on full blast, and a lady walked into the room. She started laughing with a really wicked and sinister tone that made me fearful. I started shoving my husband, in an attempt to awaken him, but he didn't move. His back was turned towards me, and his face was towards our bathroom.

As I turned him over to face me, his eyes were wide open, and he had a knot in his throat about the size of a tennis ball. I flipped him back over, grabbing him around the stomach, trying to force him to cough up what was in his throat.

When I looked up, I saw a silhouette with glowing eyes standing there. I dropped my husband, jumped under the blanket and hid my face, turning it in the opposite direction of the silhouette. With my eyes closed tight, I frantically started pinching my husband from behind, saying, "Please wake up! Please help me! I'm scared! Please get up!"

Then, I heard my sister Trina's voice saying very softly, "He can't help you; this is it. You know who to call on, call on Jesus." Immediately I opened my eyes and saw that the silhouette had jumped under the blanket and was facing me!

I jumped up, throwing the blanket off me, and stood up in the bed. Saying what I'd heard my sisters and mom say, "I rebuke you in the name of Jesus!" I said it over and over, while crying and screaming as loud as I could. I repeated it so many times I became hoarse. Each time I said it, the silhouette would back peddle slowly, then finally it disappeared.

I collapsed onto the bed, weeping uncontrollably. I called my husband name, and he said, "What is it?"

CHAPTER ELEVEN

Delivered From Fear

One afternoon I called my sister, and we had prayer together. She asked me what I wanted from the Lord. I told her I wasn't sure, but said I was hungry for Him so much so, that I couldn't sleep at night.

I worked two jobs, and while I was at work all I thought about was Jesus. I could hardly wait to get home to talk to him, or read my word.

My sister Trina was a mentor for me. I shared these experiences with her, my other sister Amanda, and my mom each time I had one. Right after prayer, she told me some music to buy.

As I played a song by Yolanda Adams, "The Battle Is Not Yours," I had a knowing that something was going to happen to me. It was my day off work, so I played that song over and over, until I made it to the deliverance service that evening.

After prayer that night, I talked with my mom on the phone for about ten minutes. Afterwards, I put a family movie in the VCR, turned the volume all the way down, and lay there for about twenty minutes trying to fall asleep.

When I turned around, we were an arm's length away from each other, and one had his arm raised as if he was about to hit me. I don't know what they saw, but they started running in the opposite direction.

I went after them, saying, "Come back so we can talk." I assured them I was not calling the police. They did come back, and I shared with them how much Jesus loved them, then made them put my groceries in my truck and gave them five dollars each. They were just teenagers.

He shared his testimony with me, saying he had $50 million dollars and lost it all, and when I saw him he was about to kill himself.

When the Holy Spirit trained me with the eyes, His purpose was to sharpen the gift of discernment He has given me. At times, I despised it, but I learned to accept His will for my life. His will is for me to walk in obedience to Him and to help His people when I'm in a position to help.

The Holy Spirit will always help you and me. He will warn us of danger, but sometimes allow us to go through things in order for His Glory to be revealed.

Some of the things we go through are to bring about righteousness in someone else's life. On the other hand, it could be a way of Him revealing Himself to us. He often uses others to warn us, or will Himself warn us.

I used to like grocery shopping at 3 a.m. My pastor asked me not to do that, but I did it anyway for years.

One night during the Christmas holidays, I decided to shop. Coming out of the store, the Holy Spirit said, "They will try to rob you." I began asking Him what to do. He said for me to keep walking and don't look back.

I heard them talking. One was saying knock her down, and the other one was saying to use the knife.

When they were about three feet away, the Holy Spirit said, "Now, turn around!"

Once I went to have a procedure done at a hospital. A doctor came in that I didn't recognize. When I looked in his eyes, I was aware he was drunk.

After he left, the doctor I was supposed to see came in to start the procedure. After I awakened, the one that was drunk was standing over me apologizing, saying he made a mistake and punctured something in my body.

After getting home, I started to vomit blood. I went to another doctor to get a body scan to try and see what I needed to do. Sure enough, he'd punctured something in my body.

The new doctor said there was no permanent damage, but it would take weeks for me to heal.

The Holy Spirit said for me to forgive him, so I did. He also said the doctor prayed and said that if I wouldn't seek recompense, he would give his life to Him.

Weeks later, I got a phone call from someone who works with that doctor, saying the doctor had changed his life.

I went to pay a bill and spotted a man the Lord showed to me in a dream. I put my truck in park, jumped out, ran up to the man who was over six feet tall, and yelled, "Suicide spirit, loose him!" He went out under the power of God, got up, gave his heart to Jesus and got filled with the Holy Ghost!"

The lady that was with him knew that about me and started praising God. He then started prophesying to her. She started screaming, then fell to the floor. He stood over her and continued to prophesy over her.

Then the Holy Spirit said, **"Stop him!"**

I yelled, "Stop!" and helped the lady up.

I looked at him and the Holy Spirit started to speak. ("I can't remember the name that was said, so I'll just call her Sue.)

I said, "Who is Sue?"

He said, "Sue who? I know a lot of people."

I said, "Sue is the lady you killed. You threw her body in the river and God has heard the prayers of her family. Hear the word of the Lord. The police now have evidence and know that you killed her. In fact, not many weeks from now they will find you. You will spend many years in jail, and in prison you will accept Jesus as your Lord.

"As you are converted, others will be converted. Now leave this town and leave God's people alone."

He said, "Okay, I'm sorry." He kept repeating, "I'm sorry, God. Please forgive me!" as he was leaving.

I shook a man's hand at a bank, looked in his eyes and asked him about how people could get loans there. He started saying without saying, (meaning he was not moving his mouth) racial slurs about a particular race of people. His words were, "I hate them! I will never help them! I know exactly what they need to do but I'm not helping them do it. I can kill all of them."

The image of satan is absolutely nothing like the way my grandma and others described him. In fact, it's the total opposite.

> And no marvel; for Satan himself will transform into an angel of light.
>
> 2 Corinthians 11:14

A friend of mine asked me to come and meet a prophet that moved to town. I told her that I would, but didn't have time that day. Subsequently, a month had gone by and different people were sharing with me, within that month, about the awesome prophecies given by that prophet.

One day, the Holy Spirit spoke to me, saying, **"Let them come."** I asked who, but He didn't respond. About ten minutes later, my phone rang and it was another lady asking me if she could come where I was because she wanted me to meet somebody. I responded yes.

After she arrived, she came in saying she wanted me to meet the prophet who'd moved to town. I walked out to meet him, and the first thing he said that got my attention was, "This lady knows God and she has to invite me." He started acting really nervous and hesitant, but appeared to be very respectful.

As he looked at the lady, he said, "Can you tell her I'm with you?" Then he looked at me and said, "You see angels?" I said yes. He then said, "You see demons, too?" I responded yes.

CHAPTER TEN

The Eyes That Covered

Over a period of time, I would see eyes, paired in different sizes and shapes. I thought this was a limited-time experience, but that was not the case. This occurred every night for an entire year.

I didn't understand it then, and certainly don't understand it fully now, but years later, it helped me in deliverance. When I look at a person, I'm able to discern what kind of deliverance that person needs. It also helps me to identify God's angels, and satan.

One night, after watching one of my favorite ministers on television, a handsome man walked in and said, "Do you know who I am?"

At first, I said no. I looked him up and down, and when I looked at his face and saw his eyes, I stopped smiling and said, "Yes, I know who you are, and you are not invited here."

He looked at the television and said, "He don't know what he's talking about."

I said, "You get out of here!" And he vanished. This was after I got delivered from the spirit of fear.

CHAPTER NINE

He's In Heaven

One night after Bible Study, I got in bed and saw myself come out of my body. I was taken up through the ceiling and into the sky. As I looked down, it was as if my ceiling rolled back, and I could see my husband and myself, lying in bed.

I stopped in midair, and before me was a massive arch with two people standing at the entrance. As I started moving toward them, I realized one of them was my boyfriend who had died. I also had a feeling that I knew the other person, but didn't know from where. We grabbed hands, all three of us in a crisscross manner. As we did so, peace filled me from within.

Afterwards, I started going back down through the sky, then through the ceiling, and then back into my body. As I sat up, the Holy Spirit said, *"The other person you saw was your son!"* My child died when he was a baby, but there he was standing five feet tall or more.

This was the day God delivered me from hurt, pain, and grief for the loss, of my child.

the garbage. The ones the Lord told me to get out of my home. My neighbor had gotten them from the trash and put them in her home, with intentions to give them away.

for the baby. My neighbor was so exhausted that she collapsed on the porch. After God brought the baby back, I laid him on the porch and ran to help my husband.

After my husband put the other child in my arms, he then dragged the man outside. They were victims of carbon monoxide poisoning. They are some of the best people I've ever met and I'm glad God spared them!

She told me while she was at work it just kept coming to her to get home early. What I learned from these experiences was to obey the Holy Spirit when He speaks, because someone's life may depend on it.

After two weeks had past, my neighbors went out of town, asking my husband to keep watch over their home, and feed the dogs.

I went to work, and received a call from my husband saying, come home quick! After arriving, saw my husband sitting in the car, watching the neighbor's house. He told me to get in the car with him, and I asked him what was going on. He said someone was in the neighbor's house. I asked how he knew, and he replied that they kept peeping out the back door. "I see their eyes, but can't tell who it is," he continued. "They keep trying to come out, but saw me sitting here."

After watching the door crack open and then close, I suggested we call the police. He asked me to sit in the car, watch who comes out the back door, and call the police. When the door opened this time, and I saw the eyes! Those were spirits! The Holy Spirit had trained me with eyes to see this. (I will share about this in the next two chapters.)

I got out of the car to go inside and get my husband, but by this time he was coming out the back door, asking, "Did they run out?"

I told him those were spirits! Walked to the back door and there were the three bags of clothing I had set out for

asked if they could come over during the week to anoint my home and pray. They agreed.

They came over Tuesday, and Amanda said, "It does feel damp in here."

Trina said gloomily, "But why?"

They suggested we sing, praise God, and anoint everything. We did, but it still felt funny. Trina said, "Let's just sit in quietness, and see if the Lord will let us know." We sat there for an hour, but got no word from the Lord.

We started to sing again, then Trina said, "Okay, ya'll, stop for a minute." She and Amanda got down on their knees in prayer, so I joined in.

Trina said, "Tina, the Lord said it's the clothes. I see clothes with tags on them. Did you buy some clothes recently?

I said, "Yes!"

She said, "He says get the clothes out of the house!"

We went through every closet got those three brands of clothing, bagged them, and set them out for the garbage. We anointed my home again, and the Presence of God returned!

That morning my neighbor asked, "What's in the bags?" I shared what happened, and she asked if she could have them. I told her no, and then explained why, then I went to work.

Thursday evening, I left for a revival out of town. Returning home after 1 a.m., I noticed two Angels standing in my neighbor's backyard. After falling asleep, I heard someone calling my name from far off.

I woke up and heard someone beating on my door, crying and screaming, "They dead, all of them! They Dead!" I opened the door, and saw it was my neighbor holding her baby that was unconscious.

I grabbed the baby, shouted for my husband to get the other family members out of the house, and started praying

ing there, wearing a white robe. He was accompanied by three small beings that flew and walked.

I said, "You are Abraham!" He smiled, as I looked at him, and I said to myself, "You are kind of young."

Aware that someone was at the window, I turned around and saw that animal looking thing peeping in. That thing said, "Open up and let me in."

Instantly, I knew God was giving me an answer about the windows. I told Abraham thank you and that it was time for me to go! On the way back, I didn't see the creatures, and the windows stopped appearing.

One Saturday evening, I decided to go shopping for my boys. After arriving at the store, I learned they had a big sale. So, I started browsing, picking out items to purchase. I heard the Lord say, **"Don't buy that."** So, I put the items back, walked around the store, then went back and picked the items back up. He said it again, **"Don't buy that."** So, I put it all back again.

Someone I knew came in, and we started talking about the sale. Before I knew it, I had my buggy filled with the same things I had just put back, plus more! And the Holy Spirit again said, **"Don't buy that!"**

I said, "This is a good sale. Why shouldn't I buy it?" I waited a while, then purchased the clothing.

Sunday morning, I got up to get ready for Church but the atmosphere in my home had changed. After I returned from Church, it was worse. I called my sisters Sunday night, and told them I didn't feel the Presence of God in my home. I

I talked to my sisters to see what they thought about it. One said maybe it was an opportunity; invite them in. I didn't think I should do that, and didn't feel good about it. So, I didn't do it, and made sure I never talked at it again. The windows continued to appear, and I continued to wait until Jesus revealed the meaning of them.

Some of my experiences were not pleasant, and some were. All of it made me feel uneasy, simply because it was happening. I was able to identify Jesus and others in heaven, but didn't know how I knew.

One night after getting in bed, I was transported in what I called at that time, space. Standing in a large building, surrounded by others, at the back of the line. As I stood there curious about what we were waiting for, peeping around the others, someone walked up and told me to come to the front.

Approaching the front, there was a big game machine, twice the size of one we see in an arcade. The man loosened the rope in front of the machine, motioning for me to come forth. I responded, saying, "I don't play video games." He then pointed to the joystick fastened on the machine.

After grabbing it, I was sucked into the screen and began flying. It was so dark, but the stars were giving off some light. All of a sudden, I saw two animal looking things out of the corner of my eye. One then flew in front of me, as though trying to scare me.

As I looked up, I saw an illuminated house with a door and a window on each side. The thought came to me that I needed to go there because Abraham lived there. As I landed on the front entrance, I opened the door. A man was stand-

I had my husband to buy me a keyboard that eventually collected dust.

Inside of me I started feeling a rumbling very forcefully as if a baby was in me turning. I could literally hear within me languages and would cover my mouth, afraid of what I would say because it was not English, the only language I spoke.

I was a carnal believer who was learning, so I interpreted things that happened in a carnal manner. When I shared it with Trina and my pastor, they told me I was grieving the Holy Spirit. After searching myself, still didn't know why I felt so uncomfortable when it would happen. But would tell God that my intentions were not to grieve Him; I just want to understand.

A year or so after, the Holy Spirit said, I had a bias with speaking in a tongue language and reminded me of an incident before I gave my heart to Jesus. He said that I felt guilty doing it because I called the police on a neighbor who was in the yard speaking in a heavenly language. As He was speaking, I was being delivered. Supernatural things started manifesting for me on a more consistent basis.

Windows of all shapes and sizes started appearing. Months had gone by, but they continued to appear.

My sisters and I researched everything we could on windows, but still no revelation on why they were appearing. One morning, I asked very loudly, "What is it about these windows?"

Someone said, "Open up and let me in."

Afterwards, I was thinking maybe I got overheated, and He was there to cool me down before I developed a high fever. But, I was not hot, nor did I feel sick.

Now, before I go any further, I just want to remind you that, I was always a scary person, and easily frighten. I depended on my husband to protect me, and to get rid of things I was afraid of. So, when I saw Him, fear came upon me, and my first instinct was to grab my husband.

After staying up all night, talking about what we saw, I couldn't wait to tell my sisters what happened. I was so relieved that my husband witnessed what I saw, because I had been telling Him things were happening to me.

Things were manifesting right before my eyes, when I would share it with him, he believed me, but didn't know what to say about them, so he wouldn't say anything. He would sit and listen to me, but had nothing to say.

After about a year later, I was at work reading while on break, and came across this scripture:

> [21]Then said Jesus to them again, "Peace be unto you: as my Father hath sent me, even so send I you." [22]And when He had said this, he breathed on them, and said unto them, "Receive ye the Holy Spirit."
>
> John 20:21-22

Supernatural things started manifesting more frequently. It seemed like the more I reached out to God, the more things happened.

For a short length of time my fingers would be moving as if I were playing an instrument, and feet patting as if I were dancing to the music I supposedly was playing. I thought that was God's way of telling me to learn to play music, so

CHAPTER EIGHT

He Blew On Me

One night after prayer, Jesus/Yeshua was standing over me, blowing on me, as He moved from side to side. He was lingering in midair, hovering over me. It startled me, so the first thing I did was grab my husband. As my husband and I sat, gazing at Him, he asked what is that, I said that's Jesus.

My husband said, "How do you know?"
I said, "I just know, but don't know how I know!"
I asked, "Do you see Him?"
He responded, "I see a light shaped like a person."
I said, "He's really real! He's a real Person!"
My husband asked, "What is He doing now?"
I responded, Blowing air on me."
He said, "Why?"
I responded, "I don't know, but I can see the air coming out of His mouth and coming upon me, cooling my body."
My husband said,"He has a mouth? I don't see a mouth."
Then He faded away.

replaying my day, I've found a lot of things I misplaced, realized that I said something wrong, and provoked a praise to God in me by just being thankful for the small things that He did throughout the day.

Although I was still afraid, it didn't stop my determination to know Him. Day and night as I sought Him through prayer and studying, His word made me realize how much I needed Him.

I wore that one dress to church for over a year, every week. Everything I spent money on to make me feel good, I got rid of. The closer I got to God, the further I moved away from things not like Him.

I started understanding more about Him and His ways. I started seeing things as they were, as opposed to what they appeared to be. The more time I spent learning about Him, the more I despised the things that had me bound. The more I loved Him, the more I hated the sin that was inside me.

I was in the prayer line every week to get totally delivered! God began showing me, as I read His word, things I needed to be delivered from. Every time I came across something I knew I struggled with, I sought God for deliverance from it. I didn't realize how bound I was until I started comparing my life to His Holy word.

Reading His word became a priority and a pleasure. I believe God used my natural father, Ligary, to discipline me to read daily as a child, so that I could use that discipline to learn about my heavenly Father, and to get my life cleaned up.

God is so smart! His plan is perfect! Every week I was getting delivered from something, but the biggest thing, which was fear, was still there. Fear was literally in charge of my life! It was the cause that produced numerous, unfavorable effects in my life. It's amazing how God does things.

Spiritual things started happening to me, on a more acute level, as my love for God grew stronger. It was like I was in another world, but in this world. My sister Trina told me to make sure I wrote down everything the Lord showed me. It reminded me of when He instructed others in His word to write down what He said, and showed them.

It's very important to write things down. Even after finishing our daily duties, as we wind down we should replay conversations we've had with others throughout the day. By

ing, and something that seemed about nine feet tall manifested, stood on the side of me, grabbed me around my neck, and dragged me several feet to the glass back door of our church.

The thing that grabbed me said, "Leave!" So I ran out and jumped into the back seat of someone's car.

As I hid, I heard my sister Amanda running around the parking lot, calling my name. I remained quiet. I was so terrified as I lay there wondering about what had just happened.

She went back into the church, got the pastor, and they came to find me. She pulled me out the car, the pastor touched my forehead, and vomit flowed from my mouth like a water faucet had been turned on.

After leaving service, I started feeling really dirty. It was as if I'd started seeing the filth that was in my life and I wanted it gone! I'd never heard of being delivered until my sister said it, but after that happened, I really wanted to be delivered. In fact, the only time I heard of the word delivered/deliverance, was in reference to a baby or receiving a package.

My being oblivious to things getting in you didn't nullify the fact of it getting in me. My being ignorant of this didn't stop it from happening. I started asking God what I needed to be delivered from, and what was it I had seen? That experience developed in me an intense hunger to be cleansed.

I took all the clothes, shoes, and purses out of my closet and put them in bags. I called my relatives and told them to come and get them. I told my husband to get all of the CDs out of my car, take the sign off the front of my car, and remove all the VCR tapes out of the house.

After removing all of my clothes and shoes, it left me with five outfits for one job, five scrub suits for the other job, and one dress.

CHAPTER SEVEN

Delivered For the First Time

After searching the scriptures diligently, crying out to God, desperate for Him to speak to me, still I had no answer. I talked with my sister Trina and Amanda daily, to get some insight on what I studied, but I was still hungry to know more.

During one of our conversations, Trina shared how God delivered her from some things and told us He wanted to do the same for us. She shared with us how she participated in deliverance services, and explained what she had to do. I didn't want to talk about that, because I was still afraid; and besides I didn't know what I needed to be delivered from.

I started going to Bible Study, Sunday service and every meeting we had. And then it began!

I was standing at the altar for prayer one Sunday. As my pastor was about to lay hands on me, my body started shak-

I believed before, but now I truly believed, and wanted to know more about what I believed. So, I began to seek God for understanding.

> Call on me and I will show you great and mighty things.
>
> Jeremiah 33:3

I would sit in my room for hours, asking God to show Himself to me, asking Him to speak to me. Sometimes, I would sit in my room hours and hours with my ears plugged listening for Him, but He didn't say a word. I would read and ask Him questions just like my sister said to do, but got no response.

Then, I began writing Him letters, telling Him how I was feeling. At that time I was still dealing with fear, and couldn't be alone, so I made sure someone was there while I sought the Lord. I wanted God to speak to me, but wanted Him to do so while someone was there, so I wouldn't be scared. I started feeling myself being drawn to know more about Him, but was still fearful of what He would say.

I started asking my husband to come to bed early, so it would give me more time to talk to God, so he did. He would actually sit up with me hours pass time he usually would go to sleep so I could pray to God longer. I had accepted Jesus/Yeshua into my heart, but was not delivered from fear as well as other things. In fact, I knew nothing about being delivered.

CHAPTER SIX

Why I Don't See Them

One Sunday, while I was sitting in church, the pastor said that angels were present recording what we gave in tithes and offerings, and the attitude in which we gave it. I said to myself, very sarcastically, "If they are here, why I don't see them?" I had my head down, looking in my purse, to get my tithe money, and I looked up and saw two angels standing there. They were more than seven feet tall, wearing bright white garments.

I said to myself, "Is this actually happening? Oh, my God! Oh, my God!" I screamed. Then I started saying, "Lord forgive me! I'm sorry!" I cried. "I didn't doubt you, I was talking to myself."

I didn't know this at the time, but when you say things to yourself, this is how you let things get in your heart. But just like we confess things to ourselves allowing it get in our hearts, we can confess them outwardly and openly to the Lord and get them out.

The two angels really got my attention! This compelled me to seek God more, and get to know Him for myself.

saved. He gave his heart to Jesus that day, and folk ridiculed him. Personally, I thought it was admirable!

At that time, I didn't understand a lot of things, but wanted to know. Spending time getting to know Jesus was a pleasure.

My sister Amanda and I spent a lot of time researching things about God. On my days off, we would sit and discuss what each of us found out. We went from drinking and smoking to sipping coffee and reading.

Amanda was always much stronger than I, and would always encourage me. Once, I was crying to her about missing my friends. She said, "Stop that crying. God will give you new friends." She inspired me so much!

Actually, she was the one who taught me how to get in the Presence of God. I would go to her home in the morning and see a sign posted on her door. "DO NOT DISTURB! IN THE PRESENCE OF GOD!"

Once, I went over there, and she didn't come out until two days later! I asked her why she stayed in so long. She said, "I was not moving until I heard Him speak." So, I started doing the same thing.

I was determined to hear Him speak to me, because I had so many questions. I wanted Him to tell me why all of those things happened to me. I wanted to know what He wanted me to do and tell me how to do it.

I remember asking Him, "Why didn't I desire You before in the way I desire You now. My mom made us go to church every Sunday and Wednesday. We even went on Tuesdays and some Saturdays. We were water baptized and very active in Church. Why didn't I know You?"

After giving my heart to Jesus, I ran across my former pastor, and asked him, "Why did you water baptize me without me being saved? Why didn't you teach me about giving my heart to Jesus and introduce me to the Holy Spirit?"

He asked for my forgiveness, and said the Lord was dealing with him concerning his life and that I was His confirmation. That week he went to a revival and told the people he preached the gospel forty years and he himself was not

> But you are a chosen people, a royal priesthood, a holy nation, a people belonging to God, that you may declare the praises of him who called you out of darkness into his wonderful light.
>
> 1 Peter 2:9

After arriving at work that day, people recognized something about me had changed. I said to them, "I got saved today, and I'm feeling something I've never felt before."

After sharing my experience, some wanted to be saved, too. So, seven of them gave their lives to Jesus that day. I just asked them to repeat after me, then said what I had heard the pastor say. I called my club buddies, and told them I had accepted Jesus and was saved. Some didn't believe me, and some said I shouldn't have done that. One said, "So, you're not going to smoke marijuana anymore?"

My answer was, "No, I don't want to."

Later, she came to pick me up, and threw a bag of marijuana to me. I said I didn't want it. She then said it was just a phase I was going through. They all laughed at me, and after weeks went by, they stopped answering my calls. Some of them would even go the other way when they saw me, in order to avoid talking to me.

By this time, my best friend, Denise, had moved out of town, and my friend, Tinka, had moved to Nashville and we didn't talk much. But Vet and I remained close. She is like a sister, and we are still good friends to this day — we're even closer, serving the Lord together.

After Denise and Tinka moved, and I'd given my life to the Lord, I didn't know what to do or where to go. I was intrigued by God, and wanted to know all about Him, just didn't know how to embrace the new life I was given in Jesus.

Then I heard it again, *"When He asks who wants salvation, you be the first one up there."*

By that time, the pastor, whom the Angel's appearance was likened to, said, "Who wants salvation?"

Immediately, I jumped up, and went to the front. I listened very carefully to what he told me to repeat, but still didn't fully understand. He then began to explain what he asked me to repeat, before praying for me. When he prayed for me, I fell to the floor. Although I had fallen to the floor a few times when he prayed for me prior to this time, at that moment it was different.

The first time he prayed for me, two other ladies were with me. He prayed for them first, and they fell to the floor. Then shortly after, I fell, got up, and said, "Do that again." He did, and I fell again. I got up, helped the other two up off the floor, and we literally ran out of the church.

We had marijuana in the car outside the church, and we smoked it and went about our business. The two ladies with me said they would never go back, but I told them that I would.

After accepting Jesus into my heart, it was as if I had stepped into another world. It was like a light was shining on the inside of me, allowing me to see everything differently. The darkness in me was now swallowed up by the Light that had moved in.

Everything within me became so illuminated, so much so that everything looked different on the outside. It was like the emptiness in me was instantly filled, giving me hope about life again.

Being overjoyed, and feeling so much peace; I instantly felt led to share with others what had happened to me.

CHAPTER FIVE

Conviction

The first week of June 2001, sitting in my home with friends, having a party, my son got his grandma to bring him home to get his game. We partied every weekend, but never in front of the children. I didn't allow any drinking, smoking or profanity around my children. In fact, my husband and I never had an argument in front of them.

However this time, my son came in where we were smoking, drinking, and using profanity. We were partying! He looked at me with tears in his eyes and said, "What's wrong with your eyes?" And ran out of the house leaving his game. I felt so bad after he ran out of the house that I made everyone leave, and then threw everything in the garbage.

After deciding to go to church the next morning, sitting on the third pew from the front I heard a voice say, ***"When he asks who wants salvation, you be the first one up there."***

I turned around to see who was speaking to me, but no one was there.

I shook a man's hand one day and knew he would go to jail for molesting children. A year later, he did. I would look at people and instantly know things about them that even I was ashamed to talk about. It had become so weird and annoying! I would know whole conversations before having them.

I saw funerals, weddings, deaths, acts of unfaithfulness, violence, children that were children in my time but saw their graduations. Also, ceremonies, parties, pregnancies, and I even saw what people would look like when they got older.

I even saw where I would be working later in life, and whom I would be working with. I saw the home I would live in, years before I purchased another home. In fact, I enjoyed the home I lived in at that time.

When I asked God to take that away from me, I remember telling Him how afraid I was. Saying, "If You love me, make it stop. I want it to STOP!!!"

the end of service a lady walked over, asking if I remembered her. I said, "No ma'am."

She called another lady over, saying. "This is the little girl we were talking about." She proceeded to tell me that she, along with other teachers, used to wait for me every morning at the school, so I could share with them what God had shown me. I had no clue what they were talking about, and to my knowledge, had never had a conversation with them.

Some of the experiences I had as a child I could remember, but most of them I could not. I'm sure they were written down, but have no idea where they are. As I became a teenager, I wrote them down, but left them at my mom's when I moved out.

One night in a dream, I saw a car leaving a bridge, and plunging into a river. In the dream, I saw a lady holding onto a tree limb with a child in her arms covered in ice, and another child in the river. I told my grandma about it, and within the next two days the event I saw in the dream made the front page of the local newspaper.

I went to my grandma crying, telling her, "I want it to stop!" She told me it was a gift from God, not to be scared. I told her I didn't want it. She then said, go to my room, get on your knees, and ask God to take it away. My grandma knew just as much as I did about God at that time, but I did what she said, and sure enough, they stopped for a season.

I didn't seem to mind the dreams that ended good, it was those that ended in death, especially the death of children, that made me despise dreaming.

Up to that point of asking God to take it away, I had so many dreams of people dying, but they were never children. There would be events where I would see who would be there, and what would go wrong.

CHAPTER FOUR

Please Take it Away

I had two best friends, one of whom was my Grandma Helen. My mom was a very hard worker, raising five children, all girls two years apart in age, so we spent a lot of time with our grandma as children.

During this time Spiritual things were happening to me that I couldn't explain, but I would share them with my grandma and my other best friend, Denise. Sometimes, it would be days before what was shown me would happen, at other times it would happen much sooner. At any rate, I would share it after seeing it, then it would manifest.

Although these things started happening to me as a child, as I began to get older, they intensified. With the many experiences I had as a child, I thought the only two who knew about them were my grandma and Denise, but apparently I shared them with a group of teachers, too.

Once after giving my life to the Lord, I went to hear a minister friend preach a service. During the service, my minister friend called out my name, asking me to stand. At

He used this supernatural experience as a way of drawing me to Him, but I didn't take heed.

Everything done in my life, I overcame from a pretense perspective, and was done by willpower, only to find out later, the Power of God could overthrow whatever had me bound, but only if I surrendered.

for Him. I saw you in a church service with lots of people and God was using you mightily. Whatever church he places you in, you should serve and remain there."

Then, he asked me what church I attended. I told him where I belonged, but told him I only attended on major holidays. He said a prayer over me, hugged me, and reminded me to give the receipt and note, to the instructor. Three days later, I received a check for $3,500!

Although I didn't know God, He knew me.

> You did not choose me, but I chose you and appointed you to go bear fruit — fruit that will last. Then the Father will give you whatever you ask in my name.
>
> John 15:16

He loved me despite the fact of me living a life of sin. I'm also reminded of this scripture:

> And we know that all things work for the good of those who love him, who have been called according to his purpose. For those he knew he also predestined to be conformed to the likeness of his Son, that he might be the firstborn among many brothers. And those he predestined, he also called; those he called, he also justified; those he justified, he also glorified.
>
> Romans 8: 28-30

Amazed and shocked about what God did, I still didn't give my life to Him. Although I learned that He speaks to people, and can solve my problems, a veil was there, blocking my understanding of Him, and knowing when He speaks.

I hadn't prayed in years, because every time I tried to pray, the enemy put thoughts in my mind like I didn't have my child or boyfriend because I prayed to God.

On that particular morning around nine o'clock, I was down on the floor praying, crying out to God, and something miraculous happened! A man appeared in my room, wearing all white, with a sash, and a belt around His waist. He was so tall, that part of His chest and the rest of Him extended through the roof. My tears dripped, and fell upon His very unusual looking feet.

He reached out His open hand, like a parent helping a child that fell, and helped me to get up. When I got off my knees, it was a few minutes after five o'clock that evening. This was my first time, talking to God that long. Most of the time, I talked *at* Him, reciting the prayer I shared in Chapter One. But, this time, it was as if He participated.

The next morning, I went to the business office, bringing along my checkbook, with the intentions of asking them to allow me to write a postdated check to delay the payment for two weeks. While waiting in line, a man came out of the inner office and called my name, asking if he could speak to me in private.

We went into another room, and he asked why I didn't have the money for my tuition. I told him I had gotten married and spent all the money on the wedding. He asked me to write down my address, telling me to stay in the room while he went to the business office.

Later, he returned with a letter and receipt, asking me to give it to my instructor when I returned to class. He then said, "I know this is strange, but the Lord showed you to me last night while you were in prayer. He told me to pay your tuition, and send you a check in three days. He also told me that He has chosen you, and that you would do great things

God's invitation that was being offered by Him through her. She would come by every week, asking me to come with her and bring the children to church. I would say, "No, I won't come, but you can take the children."

However, every time I had a problem, she was the one I called. When talking to her about my problems, she would always refer me to the Bible she gave me. I read that Bible often, but could never get past the book of Genesis.

Trina continued to explain to me how much I needed to know the God of the book of Genesis, and how I needed to accept Jesus/Yeshua into my heart and spend time with Him. She even told me I needed to tithe, and explained to me what it meant. So, I started tithing every week.

Although I was not saved, I wanted to know about God. Actually, I believed that she was saved enough for our entire family that was not, simply because she frequently prayed to God for us. My sister Trina was so devoted to interceding on our behalf and very committed to encouraging us until we accepted Jesus/Yeshua. And she didn't give up, even in those times we boldly rejected Him in her.

Being committed to college, work, and family, I didn't have time for anything else. Besides, my definition of being saved was people who wore long dresses and suits — very boring — and went to church all the time. I had no clue that God would talk to His people about people who hadn't accepted Him yet. As a matter of fact, I didn't know that He even talked to people in our day and time.

One Thursday after going to class, the instructor advised me to go to the business office. After arriving at the business office, I was told I could not go back to class until I paid my tuition for that semester. I didn't have the money, so I went home. I was on the floor, sobbing, when I remembered my sister saying I could talk to God about anything.

CHAPTER THREE

I Saw Him

⁹I, John, your brother and companion in the suffering and kingdom and patient endurance that are ours in Jesus, was on the island of Patmos because of the word of Jesus. ¹⁰On the Lord's Day I was in the Spirit, and I heard behind me a loud voice like a trumpet, ¹³and among the lampstands was someone like a son of man, dressed in a robe reaching down to his feet and with a golden sash around his chest. **¹⁴The hair on his head was white like wool, as white as snow, and his eyes were like blazing fire.** ¹⁵His feet were like bronze glowing in a furnace, and his voice was like the sound of rushing waters. ¹⁶In his right hand he held seven stars, and out of his mouth came a sharp double-edged sword. His face was like the sun shining in all its brilliance."

Revelations 1:9, 10, 13–16

My sister Trina gave me a *Women's Devotional Bible*, as a Christmas gift. She tried so very hard to get us to allow God into our lives, but we kept refusing

clubbing to drown out the pain. I started looking for pleasure while in pain, thinking if I made myself feel good the pain would go away.

I was surrounded by so many, yet was still lonely. I did things to make me feel happy, but was still sorrowful at heart. I had it together on the outside, but was torn on the inside. Each day, I saw an image of my child laying in my arms, and felt like if I could only distract myself it would go away.

I smoked marijuana daily, to help me not think about what I was thinking about, which was my child. Every day I cried out from within, wondering if someone could see me, I mean really *see me*, and pull me out of that place within myself, I called my space.

My skirts got shorter and my heels got taller. I had too much money and not enough time to spend it, so I threw it away, mostly on gambling and shopping.

reached the second or third row of seats, I waved to him. The Angel waved back, then turned into a bright light and vanished. I dropped my purse and snack bag as my mouth flew wide open from seeing what I had just seen!

In 1996, my sister Trina got married. At that time, she was a member of Triumph Church in Summit, Mississippi. Although it was a very hot afternoon, she had a beautiful ceremony. The pastor that married them was the identical appearance of the Angel that visited and sat with me to and from Chicago. I mean everything — height, weight, skin complexion, and facial features — absolutely everything about him and the Angel was the same!

I walked over to him and asked him if he remembered me, and he said no. I said, "Yes you do. We were on the same bus almost seven days together."

But he said, "No, it wasn't me."

So, I asked if he had a twin, and he said no.

I visited my sister's church on three occasions after that, and asked the pastor again if we had met prior to the wedding. He said, "No, I'm sure."

I was so embarrassed, and felt a little angry, wondering why he was pretending he didn't know me after I had shared all my woes, hurts, and concerns with him. I told my sister about it. She just laughed, and began to feel ashamed herself, forbidding me to ask him about it again.

My life at that point had begun to take a drastic turn. I felt like I was slowly sinking into a hole, struggling with each breath. I started smoking marijuana, gambling, drinking, and

dow, saying to myself repetitively, "Please don't let him sit with me."

He bypassed all the empty seats, and asked, *"May I sit with you?"*

I replied, with hesitation, "Yes."

He then said, *"I'm here to listen and encourage you."* He grabbed my hand, saying, *"Now tell me all about it. All of it!"*

As He grabbed my hand, a warm sensation came over me. So, naturally, I began sharing with him everything that happened — about my child dying, and six months later my child's father dying.

His very frequent response to my dilemmas was, *"God loves you."*

We were together on the bus for almost three days, during which time I did most of the talking. We arrived in Chicago on Thanksgiving morning. The Angel walked with me, carrying my luggage as I exited the bus. He then said, *"I will see you later."*

I asked him where his destination was and he said, *"Further north."*

After arriving at my sister's, I found out she was hospitalized. When I realized her family did not celebrate Thanksgiving, I decided to return home. As I got on the bus, the same man reappeared and sat with me again. He listened as I talked and cried.

Again, his response always was, *"God loves you."*

I asked to buy him food several times, but he politely refused. I reminded him that, he didn't eat on the bus to Chicago either, and I asked, "So, you're still not hungry?" He smiled and then offered to go get me some food.

After arriving back in McComb that Sunday, he unloaded my bags and luggage, then he got back on the bus. When he

CHAPTER TWO

Angel on the Bus

Are not all angels ministering spirits sent to serve those who will inherit salvation?

Hebrews 1:14

For he will command his angels concerning you to guard you in all your ways.

Psalm 91:11

After the funeral, I relapsed into deep depression. So, in November 1992, the week of Thanksgiving, I packed everything I had and caught the bus that Tuesday for Chicago, where my oldest sister Amanda lived.

While sitting on the bus, in somewhat of a daze, waiting to depart the depot, I prayed that when it pulled out, I would be leaving all the hurt and pain behind me.

Suddenly, a man walked onto the bus. Somehow, I knew he was an angel, and I knew he was there for me. As he began walking down the aisle, I started looking out the win-

long. The hearing is one of the last things to leave a person. Do it now! You can do it."

So, I went into his room, placed my lips very close to his ear, and told him what my mother told me to say. Tears rolled from his eyes, trickled down his cheekbone, and about thirty minutes later, he died.

On the way back home, thoughts entered my mind concerning my son Corneilius. I wondered if I should tell him when I arrive, or if the news would affect him in a negative way. Would he even understand, or should I wait and tell him later?

I started telling myself, "You are strong! Be strong for your son. Don't let him see you cry, he's only a child. Prepare yourself for the other family members; they will need you. Whatever you do just don't fall apart!" But when I saw his sister Vet, who is my friend and is like my sister even to this day, I FELL APART!

After analyzing my situation, I came to the realization that I needed to make a change. So, I decided to move out of the state.

When we were about thirty feet from the hospital, we saw three of his cousins running towards the car, screaming and telling us to get out of the car. I asked what was wrong, though I had gotten the news, I just didn't know how serious it was. Actually the thought never crossed my mind that he would never recover. After asking them what was wrong, one of them answered, "He shot my cousin in the head!"

Suddenly, I couldn't hear again. Everything had gone numb, and an eerie silence filled the still atmosphere. I was in the midst of hundreds of people, yet I could not hear the people that were there or my Aunt Kathy talking to me. *I could not hear them!*

My mom worked at the hospital during that time, so she was allowed to go in the room with his mom. As my Aunt Kathy put both hands on my shoulder, it seemed as if she was moving in slow motion. I tried reading her lips, but couldn't.

Shortly after, my mom walked towards me, carrying the blood-drenched sweater they had cut off him! When she stood in front of me, I could hear her! *I could hear her!* My mom's voice was the *only* voice I could hear. She said, "Tina, he's not going to make it. He has coded twice and is on life support." At that moment, I could suddenly hear everybody and everything!

Soon, he was airlifted to the state hospital, and soon after, I arrived there as well. My mom called me on the waiting room pay phone, telling me to go into his room and whisper in his ear that he should ask God to forgive him, and then let him go and be with Jesus.

I screamed and hung the phone up on her. That was like asking God to let him die!

My mom called back about three times, and each time she called, I would hang up on her. Finally, the last time she called, she said, "He is *not* going to make it. You don't have

Afterwards, he asked me if I forgave him, and I responded with a "yes." As he often did, he called me "Ms. Pretty" and told me to take care of our son Corneilius, who at that time was only three years old. He kissed me on the cheek, and walked off down the driveway. As I watched him walk away, I wondered what was wrong with him. Then, he turned and blew me a kiss.

After finishing with my clients, I rode to the store with a friend. Nearby I saw my boyfriend stooped down, talking to a couple of his friends, who were sitting in their car. When we got about 20 feet from him, I couldn't hear anything. Our eyes locked, and everything seemed to move in slow motion.

The children were out playing on both sides of the street, the music was blasting in my friend's truck, but I couldn't hear them or the music. As we approached my boyfriend, he rose up, seemingly in slow motion, and waved goodbye to me. I began waving back at him, until we reached the stop sign a short distance from where he was.

Only then could I hear the music, the children playing, and the noise from the heavy traffic! My friend asked me if I was okay. I said yes, but couldn't explain what had just happened. I only knew it was strange.

After leaving the store, I asked my friend to go back the same way, but my boyfriend was gone.

Later that night, I went to my best friend's mother-in-law's home to help take care of her and her husband. (They were the two in the bad car wreck that my boyfriend walked away from with no injuries. She and her husband both suffered broken pelvic bones.) While I was there, my boyfriend's sister came and picked up my son, but returned about fifteen minutes later with the news that her brother (my boyfriend) had been shot.

My mom took really good care of me during that time. She would spoon-feed me small amounts of food while I lay in bed, lovingly and gently blowing in my face, as a way of encouraging me to swallow the food. She and my grandma did everything they could to make me feel better.

During the first week of October 1992, I came out of depression, and began interacting with my friends, going to the clubs, and setting appointments for my clients. However, I hadn't been to my apartment in months, and had no desire to return to it, or my previous life.

My boyfriend would come to my mom's to check on me, and our son Corneilius. Although my boyfriend and I came to a mutual agreement that we would not live together or be together anymore, he was determined to help me get my life back on track.

At the end of September 1992, my boyfriend, my best friend and her husband, and two other persons were in a bad car accident. Traveling at about 60 mph, the car crashed into a tree. The force of the impact wrapped the car around the tree, dislodging the engine from the car and propelling it to the opposite side of the street. My boyfriend, who was the only one not injured, pulled everyone out of the wreckage.

On October 17, 1992, around 6 a. m., my boyfriend washed all my mom's windows inside and out, shampooed the carpet, and cleaned out my closet. After he finished, he asked me to walk him to the door.

As we stood in the doorway, he turned and gave me some papers, and told me they were very important papers and to put them in a safe place because I would need them. He then took $20 out of his weekly pay and gave me the rest. He asked me to forgive him for everything he had ever done against and to me.

tongue hanging from its mouth, as if it gagged and choked, devastated me. I started screaming, "What's wrong with my child?"

The doctor said, "I'm sorry, ma'am, your child has expired."

I shouted, "What do you mean? Please! Please, sir, help us!"

He said, "I'm sorry, ma'am, there is nothing else I can do."

I shouted, "My child is dead? Please, someone help us!" As my child lay in my arms I started shouting, "What went wrong? Oh, my God! What happened to my baby?"

After a while, they tried to take my baby from my arms. I started yelling, "Please don't take my baby!" as I gripped my child tighter. As they were taking my baby, I started pushing them away. They called someone in to strap me down, and to give me medicine to calm me.

At that point I had became so angry, yelling, "Someone, *please!* Someone stop them from taking my baby away!" Then, I started to feel relaxed and dozed off.

The death of my baby caused me to sink into a deep state of depression. I was so overwhelmed with grief, I couldn't think of anything but my child. I felt so empty inside and was beyond exhausted. I was filled with so much rage and so much hurt, there was no fight in me for life during that time.

I remember telling God to keep everybody away from me, and vowed to never leave my mom's house again. I also frequently asked Him, "Why did You take my baby?"

I was so overwhelmed with depression and felt so empty inside. I didn't want to be in a relationship with my boyfriend anymore, and prayed to God every night to keep him and others away from me. In fact, I didn't want to work, eat, sleep, socialize with others, or watch TV.

moment of the break-in, I concluded it frighten me because my mom was crying and wore a fearful look upon her face.

It was this incident that opened the door to fear in my life! That night was when the spirit of fear entered into me. Fear invaded me, and I was so overwhelmed from that experience that it affected almost every decision I made! The spirit of fear had bound me beyond my childhood, to the degree that I was afraid to drive at night, afraid of bugs, afraid of being alone, and afraid of being afraid. Fear tormented and tormented me for years!

For my sake I was seldom left alone. Most of the time, my sisters were home with me or we were at my grandparents in Baertown, a small community were we grew up and had once lived prior to moving to Burgland, another city across town. After moving to Burgland we still spent most of our days with our grandparents and other relatives, because my mom worked long hours.

I lived with fear from that time until I gave my life to the Lord/Yeshua and allowed Him to fill me with His Holy Spirit.

> I indeed baptize you with water unto repentance: but he that cometh after me is mightier than I, whose shoes I'm not worthy to bear: he shall baptize you with the Holy Ghost and with Fire.
>
> Matthew 3:11

In April 1992, before Jesus saved me, I gave birth to a child who died, and a part of me died also. As I held the lifeless body of my baby in my arms, looking at my child's

Again, as simple as that prayer may seem, it spared my life.

One windy and cool night, as I lay gazing at the ceiling, my window began to flap. I looked towards it and saw someone in the shadows looking back at me. Happy to see them, I helped to pull them through the window. After entering my bedroom, the person picked me up, gave me the biggest, warmest hug, and carried me into my mom's bedroom.

The house in which we lived had lights attached to the wall, and the only way to turn them on was to twist the knob at the base. As that person fumbled with the light switch, my mom awoke suddenly, reached for her gun with the intention of firing it, as soon as the light illuminated the room.

As soon as the light was turned on, she saw the person holding me and began to cry uncontrollably. My mom knew the person and had no idea that they would break into our home. I, on the other hand, didn't know it was a break-in. Mother told me years later after that happened, that she was crying out to God, thanking Him for preventing her from seriously injuring me or killing me.

Although the person fled the scene, she was grateful that I was not harmed.

After accepting Jesus/Yeshua into my heart, I started asking Him for answers concerning my life. Among my biggest concerns was: Why have I always been afraid? After my mother reminded me of that particular incident, memories began to flood my mind, and I especially remembered how I felt seeing the fright and devastation in her countenance on the night of the break-in.

Before accepting Jesus/Yeshua as my Lord and Savior, I used to tell my family, "When you see me worried, you should be concerned," but now I say, "If you see me concerned, you should pray!" After realizing how I felt at the

I said, "I can't get on Big Joe! I will fall." Big Joe was the family dog.

By that time, we heard the men coming on the three-wheelers. I jumped on Big Joe, grabbing him around the neck, with my eyes closed as tight as I could get them.

My cousin shouted, "Come on, boy!" Big Joe took off with me on his back, with my arms wrapped around his neck. I rode him for almost two miles, back to my cousins' home, and got off of him under their carport.

This is one of the many times I prayed to God this simple prayer and He provided protection for me by supernatural means.

As a child even younger than when I was chased by the men on the three-wheelers, I was always afraid — scared of people, animals, scary movies, but mainly afraid of death. I didn't understand why I was so afraid of everything and certainly didn't know how to overcome it, so I just dealt with it the best I knew how.

Fear had such a grip on my life that it influenced and manipulated every decision I made, until the Lord freed me from its vicious hold.

> [14]Since the children have flesh, he too shared in their humanity so that by his death he might destroy him who holds the power of death — that is the devil — [15]and free those who all their lives were held in slavery by their fear of death.
>
> Hebrews 2:14, 15

As simple as this prayer may seem, it spared my life on numerous occasions. On one particular occasion, at the age of 9, my cousins and I decided to go on an adventure one hot summer day, though we'd been warned numerous of times by my grandma and other relatives not to go to this particular place. After arriving at the place we witnessed something horrific and were spotted by some of the men on three-wheelers. My cousin Kevin told us to split up, in an attempt to lure the men away from us girls.

All of us were riding our bikes going through the woods but unfortunately mines was slowing me down, so I got off it and started to run, but were separated from the others. I heard the men getting closer as they hurled insults and made bets on which one would catch me first to do me bodily harm. One of the men spotted me and got off his three-wheeler to chase me on foot. I crouched down behind a patch of bushes and started reciting that prayer over and over. As he got closer I panicked, jumped up, and hid behind an oak tree, still reciting that prayer.

When about five feet in front of me, still even closer, though looking right at me, he walked past me as though I was invisible. He started saying, I know you are here, come out wherever you are." He then started using profanity saying what he would do to me when he caught me. After his voice started fading, I ran as fast as I could in the opposite direction. After running and hiding, I was lost in the woods for about an hour. As I came to a body of water behind a field, I peeped out and saw some of my cousins, and started running towards them frantically! They were there waiting on their bikes.

My cousin Kevin asked me, "Where is your bike?" I told him I left it in the woods. He then said, "Get on Big Joe."

CHAPTER ONE

Fear Entered In

*"Now I lay me down to sleep,
I pray the Lord my soul to keep.
Guard me Jesus through the night,
and wake with the morning light.
Amen."*

This was a prayer framed on my bedroom wall that I prayed nightly as a child. My mom hung this framed prayer and instructed my sisters and me to get on our knees every night before bed, and recite this prayer so that God could protect us.

On nights I couldn't go to sleep, I would say it over and over until I drifted off. Despite the fact that I didn't have a personal relationship with God, it was instilled in me that God could protect me, so I believed He would if I prayed it. Although I prayed this prayer mainly out of fear, it gave me a sense of peace and comfort knowing I said it.

ing in my bedroom in front of the television. I stood there puzzled, wondering how I would start.

He whispered, *"Just start writing. Write the book! Write the book!!"*

As I began the process, I was reminded of what my sister Trina shared with me, saying Jesus wanted me to write down every experience I would have in Him during the years to come because He would later use them for His Glory. The relief I felt when He gave me the instructions to share those experiences was likened to air seeping from a balloon.

Often I would ask Him what was His purpose for showing what was being revealed to me. Now that I've learned His purpose, it makes the process, in a sense, beyond worth it.

In this book, I will often refer to Jesus as Yeshua, His Hebrew name. He has many names and titles, but this one, Yeshua, is very, personal to me, for many reasons. For instance, when I utter "Yeshua," instantly, I feel His Presence. The atmosphere I stand in at that moment becomes my reality.

Throughout my life, as the Holy Spirit revealed Him to me, I've become acquainted with His Person. The privilege of knowing Him has brought me into a deeper revelation of who He is.

This book is not written in a chronological manner! Some of the experiences are very detailed, others are short and to the point, but methodically arranged as pertaining to the experience.

In the spring of 2015, after going to sleep, I awakened to find myself in a large, multi-level building. The floors were marble squares, with walls as white as light. As I stood there gazing, an Angel appeared and said, "Follow me."

As I followed, we approached another room, with a person seated in the center of the room, at a table with sheets of papers spread over it. When we approached the table where the Person was, He looked at me and said, **"Countina, you are to write a book, sharing with My people the experiences you have in Me. This is My will and purpose for your life. Don't be afraid to share, I'm with you. Many will desire a deeper relationship with Me as a result of the book."**

I motioned my head as if to say, "Okay." He smiled, and then I started moving back towards the door.

The Angel that was leading me was, at this point, walking behind me. After we entered the next room, the Angel touched my shoulder from behind, and then I was stand-

love him"— ¹⁰but God has revealed it to us by his Spirit. The Spirit searches all things, even the deep things of God. ¹¹For who among men knows the thoughts of a man except the man's spirit within him.? In the same way no one knows the thoughts of God except the Spirit of God. ¹²We have not received the spirit of the world but the Spirit who is from God, that we may understand what God has freely given us. ¹³This is what we speak, not in words taught us by human wisdom but in words taught by the Spirit, expressing spiritual truths in spiritual words. ¹⁴The man without the Spirit does not accept the things that come from the Spirit of God, for they are foolishness to him and he cannot understand them because they are spiritually discerned.

1 Corinthians 2:9-14 (NIV)

The Holy Spirit is the only One who relays the groanings we have inwardly, to the Father. He's also the only One who could translate those groanings to us. Once while studying about Jesus's crucifixion, I asked the Holy Spirit why was Jesus's words few on the cross?

He replied, **"What the people heard were few words, but He said much more than that through groanings, would you like me to translate?"**

I said, "Yes!"

He responded, **"They heard, Father forgive them; for they know not what they do. I thirst. Women, behold thy Son! Behold thy mother!**

Verily I say unto thee, today shalt thou be with Me in paradise. Eli, Eli, lama sabachthani? Father, into thine hands I commend My Spirit: It is finished: But He groaned inwardly, read Psalm 22."

With many of these testimonies and experiences, the Holy Spirit has given me insight as to the meaning, and some are just unexplainable. For example, each time I met with Jesus (Yeshua), we talked, but our mouths were not moving. Also during these encounters and conversations, someone else is there impacting our conversation, though I could not see Him.

> ...with groanings which cannot be uttered...
>
> Romans 8:26

Groaning and moaning are two different acts, but closely related. One can be heard and one cannot. Groanings are silent.

Groanings are the communication of God the Father, God the Son, and God the Holy Spirit. This could be done in the inner being of the believer or apart from him or her. Not only do we as humans groan inwardly, the whole creation groans.

> [22] We know that the whole creation has been groaning as in the pains of childbirth right up to the present time. [23] Not only so, but we ourselves, who have the first fruits of the Spirit, groan inwardly as we wait eagerly for our adoption to sonship, the redemption of our bodies.
>
> Romans 8:22, 23 (NIV)

The Holy Spirit is the one who relays groanings we have to the Father. He alone understands it. 1 Corinthians confirms this:

> [9] No eye has seen, no ear has heard, no mind has conceived what God has prepared for those who

Introduction

Experiencing The Supernatural Life is a collection of testimonials and experiences written in a book. It's not only a book I've written, but one I live.

The biblical meaning of supernatural is being above or beyond what is natural; abnormal, as pertaining to the characteristics of God or a deity.

The Supernatural is likened to a natural man becoming a spiritual man, a person born of water and the Spirit. The Spiritual man relies on the wisdom of God, the natural man relies on human wisdom.

What is nature is natural, what's above nature is supernatural. When the word natural is connected to another word it's in agreement to what it's attached to. When the word super is attached to another, it adds more to what it's connected to.

In this book are testimonials and experiences I've had throughout my life. Some I understand, others I do not, but many have been revealed through the word of God.

Daniel 9:2 says, In the first year of his reign, I, Daniel, understood from the scriptures, according to the word of the Lord given Jeremiah the prophet…"

Table of Contents

Introduction ix

Chapter One	Fear Entered In...............................	1
Chapter Two	Angel On The Bus	11
Chapter Three	I Saw Him	15
Chapter Four	Please Take It Away	21
Chapter Five	Conviction......................................	25
Chapter Six	Why I Don't See Them	31
Chapter Seven	Delivered for the First Time............	33
Chapter Eight	He Blew On Me	37
Chapter Nine	He's in Heaven	45
Chapter Ten	The Eyes That Covered	47
Chapter Eleven	Delivered From Fear.......................	53
Chapter Twelve	Ask Me for What You Want............	59
Chapter Thirteen	Amina...	65
Chapter Fourteen	Show Me Your Glory......................	69
Chapter Fifteen	He Jumped In	73
Chapter Sixteen	Angels Galore.................................	77
Chapter Seventeen	It is I...	85
Chapter Eighteen	In His Presence	89
Chapter Nineteen	Intimacy Beyond Ecstasy	95
Chapter Twenty	Kidneys from Heaven.....................	109
Chapter Twenty-One	Who is That Lady?..........................	119
Chapter Twenty-Two	She Will Be Changed......................	123
Chapter Twenty-Three	A Seer Sees What I'm Doing...........	129
Chapter Twenty-Four	Ministry of the Holy Spirit..............	133
Chapter Twenty-Five	It's Real! It's Real!	137
Chapter Twenty-Six	The Ultimate Invitation..................	141

Dedication

To Yeshua (Jesus), who saved me, and filled me with His Holy Spirit.

My husband Jeffery Spurlock and children; Corneilius, Jeffory, Amina and Asher.

To my pastor and overseer, Dr. Rufus Rawls whom God chose to watch over, and train me in righteousness.

The Administration of the Holy Spirit prayer group, Evangelist Dorothy Jones, Shelia Hughes, Diane Nunnery, Nicole Irvine, Vicky Luckett, Anita Matthews, Letisha Harris, Scherry Martin, Tomekia Luckett, Jeanette Young, Sandra Pittman, Lytoria Miller, Meaghan Johnson, Tamara Brister, Shonta Coney, Shenitha Davis, Miko Butler, Deidre Reese, Erica Patton, Sharon Morris, Leigha Martin, and Abigayl Thomas.

© 2018, Tina Spencer Spurlock

All rights reserved.

No portion of this book may be reproduced, stored in a retrieval system, or transmitted in any form or by means—electronic, mechanical, photocopy, recording, scanning, or other excerpt for brief quotations in critical reviews or articles, without prior written permission of the publisher.

ISBN: 978-1-948638-86-9

All scripture references are quoted from
NIV and KJV Bibles

Published by

Fideli Publishing, Inc.
119 W. Morgan St.
Martinsville, IN 46151

www.FideliPublishing.com

Experiencing The Supernatural Life

A Collection of Testimonials and Experiences

TINA SPENCER SPURLOCK

Countina Spurlock is like the best big sister I've ever had. She's my mentor, friend, and one of the most pure in heart women of God I have ever met. I met her years ago and meeting her has changed my life forever. She directed me straight into the arms of Jesus/Yeshua.

She's very strict concerning God's business, and firmly believes in empowering His people.

Countina has taught and shown me so many things in my walk with God, without her I don't know where I would be today. Her prayers, teachings, and obedience to the Holy Spirit have been a great blessing to me.

Two of the greatest things she had done for me were: one, introducing me to the Holy Spirit, and His ministry; and two, inviting me into the prayer ministry. The prayer ministry is filled with so many awesome God loving individuals. When we meet, His Presence becomes so rich among us, as His love pours out upon us. We strive to help others under the leading of the Holy Spirit, no matter what it takes. She is full of love, encouragement, and fellowships with God in His Presence. The miracles that have taken place under the ministry are mind blowing.

—LeTisha Harris

Countina Spurlock is a true warrior! Usually when one imagines a warrior, one likely visualizes a helmet, sword, breastplate, and armor. When I imagine a warrior, I visualize Countina. She is quiet, humble, and compassionate; yet, powerful, strong, and tenacious. The very forces of evil tremble when she enters into an atmosphere. I have watched her slay colossal giants through the power of the Holy Ghost. Her demonstration of faith is evident as she lays hands on the sick, and they recover. She speaks to the mind and soul issues, which have led many into captivity and years of unspoken bondage.

Through her unique gifting through eye contact, she can see a person's condition, and help them be free from issues they may or may not know exist. My warrior does not wear physical armor, but shows up in heels, dresses, and with the full power of the Holy Ghost! *HE* IS HER ARMOR!

— Dr. Tomekia Luckett

Expressions about Tina Spencer Spurlock (also known as Countina):

This book *Experiencing The Supernatural Life* is just that; reading it is an experience in the Supernatural. Countina Spurlock's close walk with God is so powerful, personal and genuine, that everyone who reads this book will hunger and thirst for more of God. Her experiential walk with God is one that will inspire you to know that God desires to use His people and transform their lives, as well as the lives of others they are connected to. Moreover, I can personally attest to a number of her testimonial experiences, that you are about to read, because I've been given the privilege by God to pastor her. In all the books I have read, I can't remember a single one in which every word, line, sentence, paragraph, and page is overflowing with the presence of God.

—Dr. Rufus Rawls,
Pastor of Triumph Church, Summit, Miss.,
Author of *The Perfect Thinker*

Countina Spurlock is a friend, teacher, prophet, God-led, Spirit-filled, and committed to God's people saint; these are only a few of her characteristics and titles that are inherent to who she is. Tina is one of the original founders/organizers of The Administration of the Holy Spirit, a member of Triumph Church in Summit, Ms., under the leadership of Dr. Rufus Rawls, and one of the founders of Open Your heart Testimonial Group 2.0.

She has led many to Jesus, assisted in them being filled with the Holy Spirit and helped them to gain a greater understanding of God's word. She has shared revelations given her by the Holy Spirit through teachings, testimonies and impartations.

Countina gives her all to the service of God. Serving His people, not based on who they are but who they will become. She sees people as God sees them.

God honors her and showers her with His favor.

—Minister Scherry Martin